NATURE CHRONICLES OF INDIA

Ananda Banerjee is a conservation journalist, graphic designer and fine art photographer. Being an avid birder, he has authored books like the best-selling *Common Birds of the Indian Subcontinent* and *Wild Trail in Madhya Pradesh*, and has also been a contributing author for the book, *Birds and People*.

A FEJI-ATREE media fellow, he has contributed to several books, magazines, galleries and museums around the globe. He writes on natural history conservation in *Mint* and has been associated with the Centre for Science and Environment (*Down To Earth* magazine), India Today Group, *The Pioneer*, Peace Institute, ELDF (Environment, Law and Development Foundation), National Tiger Conservation Authority and Global Tiger Forum. He was a nomination jury member for 'Vatavaran'—India's Environment and Wildlife Film Festival (2003 & 2013) and is a merit awardee, AEJA Environmental Journalist of the year 2014.

NATURE CHRONICLES
OF INDIA

essays on wildlife

edited by

Ananda Banerjee

RUPA

First published by
Rupa Publications India Pvt. Ltd 2014
7/16, Ansari Road, Daryaganj
New Delhi 110002

Sales centres:
Allahabad Bengaluru Chennai
Hyderabad Jaipur Kathmandu
Kolkata Mumbai

ISBN: 978-81-291-3487-5

First impression 2014

10 9 8 7 6 5 4 3 2 1

The moral right of the authors has been asserted.

Typeset by Saanvi Graphics, Noida

Printed at Gopsons Papers Ltd., Noida

*Dedicated to late Mr Rinchen Wangchuk
and Mr Arun Bakshi*

Contents

SECTION TWO: FROM THE ARCHIVES

Introduction

Nature works in mysterious ways. After thousands of years of human exploration and colonization, new species are still stumbling out of the woods every year. The world of natural history is a fascinating one. It has inspired the human race to observe and study other species which share this planet. It is an endless quest for discovery.

Historical records of natural history in India date back to the Indus Valley Civilization, one of the world's earliest urban civilizations (3300–1300 BC). It was through the excavation of seals and pottery that we came to know of the presence of wild animals in those flourishing times. The Vedas, the oldest text of Hinduism, recorded a wealth of flora and fauna between 1700 BC and 500 BC. Further on, successive empires like the Mauryan, Chalukyan and Mughal have recorded natural history in the form of court gifts, royal hunts and private game reserves for respective kings. Emperors such as Ashoka, Babur and Jehangir were amongst the first to lay down conservation rules and maintained detailed records of forests and wildlife in their personal journals.

The process of documenting modern natural history in India started with the colonization of the country by the British. During the 200 years of British rule, hunting was a way of life for officers and the aristocracy. Some of them were gifted writers who recorded their wild exploits and expeditions. They were hunters who made notes on species that roused their curiosity, even sending specimens back to England for identification.

Before the British East India Company, the oldest book on natural history in India was published by the Dutch. *Hortus Indicus Malabaricus* by Hendrik Van Rheede (1636–91) was the first book on flora for the Malabar region (present-day Kerala).

The interest in natural history among the British had a direct impact on the subcontinent and the Indian Civil Services facilitated in bringing many such naturalists to India from Britain. A growing number of such naturalists and nature enthusiasts led to the founding of the Bombay Natural History Society (BNHS) in 1883 to document and share knowledge on Indian wildlife.

Though *The Jungle Book* (1894) by novelist Rudyard Kipling remains the most popular account of Indian wildlife today, there are many others from that era who were pioneers in their chosen subject and have enriched our understanding of species and their respective habitats.

William Thomas Blanford, Edward Charles Stuart Baker, Edward Lockwood, Colonel William Henry Sykes, Edward Hamilton Aitken, Allan Octavian Hume, Thomas Caverhill Jerdon, Edward Percy Stebbing, Captain James Forsyth, Ferdinand Stoliczka, Hugh Whistler, Robert and Charles Swinhoe, George Peress Sanderson, Douglas Dewar, Edward Blyth, Samuel Tickell and Frank Finn are a few stalwarts who made natural history an engaging subject through their writings in scientific and popular journals.

Among these men, Allan Octavian Hume (1829–1912)—one of the founders of the Indian National Congress was also known as the Father of Indian Ornithology. Within a span of ten years (1872–82) Hume had gathered an unrivalled collection of Indian birds from all parts of the country. He accumulated 60,000 skins besides a large collection of bird eggs and nests which he donated to the British Museum.

The Indian Forest Act came into existence in 1865 and was later consolidated in 1927. We follow this 148-year-old act even today. It was only in 1972 that the Wildlife Protection Act came into force with overriding powers in the Indian Forest Act for the protection and management of wildlife in India. This was a game changer in wildlife conservation after hunting was banned in 1968.

Today, natural history books are few and far between. Old books are mostly archived in libraries and museums without easy access for everyday reading. While the works of Jim Corbett and Rudyard Kipling have stood the test of time as popular literature, others were lost in time. The present generation is yet to draw from the wonderful literature of these great natural history writers.

So, why this book?

This book is an attempt to revive some of the fine writings from the colonial period which have inspired many modern-day naturalists. The book is divided into two sections. The first section features writings on seven modern researches in wildlife conservation from the Indian subcontinent. The second section consists of diverse stories by seven British wildlife writers.

These writings, especially those from the past, will transport you to the forests and landscape of yore. There are interesting records of the forest and lives of people in British India. The stories tell us about a flourishing wildlife, jungles packed with wild animals, and backyards and kitchen gardens teeming with common species.

Given the vastness of the subject and fascinating tomes left by a huge number of past writers, it is not an easy task to pick a few. Where do you begin? How do you choose one over the other? After all, they are all records of a rich past we have inherited. A perplexing task, nonetheless, I have tried to showcase a few of my favourite authors whose works have influenced me. Among the modern-day writers, I have chosen those whose work unveils lesser-known species, not commonly discussed. In this section, film-makers, journalists and scientists share their field experiences. Bringing a range of stories from the heart of action: where communities get involved in wildlife conservation, up-close with elusive and endangered species such as the Asiatic wild dog and the snow leopard; getting to know sea turtles; adventures in researching the bonnet macaque, the commonest monkey in South India; and a peek into the fascinating world of birds and their importance in ecology.

Ananda Banerjee

SECTION ONE:

CONTEMPORARY WRITINGS

Community Conservation: A Work in Progress[*]

JAY MAZOOMDAAR

It is an exhilarating sight: just 5 centimetres long and weighing less than 20 grams, the tiny turtles struggle to emerge from the sand. Surfacing in groups (they find it easier to dig their way out en masse), the newborns take a moment to orientate themselves—after all, the females will have to return to this beach to lay their own eggs in ten or fifteen years' time. Their eyes still sealed by sand, they make their way instinctively towards the sea, their fins leaving ripples down the beach. The moment they enter the water, their translucent, feature-light carapaces turn dark. The first wave swells, lifts the hatchlings and drops them right back on the beach. Nature's first lesson learnt, the little ones dive straight into the surging waves and disappear.

It's an exhilarating sight and it cannot be rushed.

---

[*] A version of this article first appeared in *Condé Nast Traveller* magazine in 2013.

It is my third evening in Velas with photographer Sandesh Kadur. The weekend crowd has disappeared. On the beach, tourists number less than a handful of the volunteers who are about to perform the ritual that stirs up just enough excitement this last-mile village can handle. For several days now, volunteers from Sahyadri Nisarga Mitra (SNM), a local conservation NGO, have been visiting their turtle hatchery twice, soon after sunrise and just before sunset, to check if the eggs have hatched.

The beach at Velas, a village on the Konkan coast some 200 kilometres south of Mumbai, is one of the few remaining hatching sites of the endangered olive ridley turtle in India. Here, they do not appear in their thousands like on the Odisha coast, but of all the beaches on the western coast, Velas is their favourite—about 1000 newborn turtles take off from its shores each season. Now, the area is gaining a reputation for turtle tourism, after a festival set up by SNM has helped raise awareness on the olive ridleys and their lifecycle.

During the breeding–nesting season, which runs from November to February at Velas, volunteers from SNM collect eggs from turtle nests along this 2.5-kilometre beach. Then they put them in artificial nests buried in the sand within a fenced-in patch of beach, where the eggs are safe from predators and poachers. After the eggs incubate for fifty or sixty days, the hatchlings emerge and are released into the sea.

Velas has been witnessing this magical lifecycle for generations, so the villagers know that the eggs cannot be rushed. But, for visitors, the wait for the turtles to hatch can be frustrating. As we wait, not one single hatchling has surfaced in the last six days and a couple of nests are overdue.

Odds in its favour, the crowd surrounding the turtle enclosures wait expectantly, cameras cocked. The volunteers arrive to conduct their evening inspection. It is a brief, solemn routine. They enter the enclosure, go down on their knees and remove the cane baskets placed over the nests as protection. The sand reveals that there has been a slight commotion underground but nothing more.

The volunteers look a little apologetic. The day before, a bunch of impatient youngsters had heckled them when the hatchlings failed to play to a handsome weekend turnout. 'You keep saying they are overdue. Just perform a Caesarean, guys!' one tourist yelled. Today, though, the visitors disperse quietly; except for two young men from a neighbouring village, who seem to be fascinated by the hatchery.

They discuss the sticks with tiny labels marking each nest and its gestation span, and stop at the ropes and the orange plastic cones the volunteers use to cordon off people when the hatchlings waddle to the sea. 'These (cones) are put on roads during construction work. Remember those signs? *Kaam chaalu aahe* (work in progress).'

Left with that reassuring metaphor, I walk towards the advancing breakers—it's not often you get an entire beach to yourself at sunset, after all.

2

For seven years now, this tiny Konkan village is a destination during the turtle season. Velas is happy with the attention but not easily excited. The elderly host at our homestay sits in front of the TV all day. The widower's young son runs errands, and the show, with a slow smile. Two whispering village girls run the kitchen. Shoes are not allowed inside. Pups prance around a fenced well in the backyard. Even the hunting dogs play without a noise.

In the front, the road snoozes in the sun. A short, young labourer does continuous rounds carrying areca nut saplings, one at a time, from a nursery across the road to a plantation field beyond the backyard. Outside the first-floor windows, betel nuts bake in the sun on an asbestos roof. From my room, I can hear a coppersmith barbet, until other guests, a cackling group of friends from Mumbai, move into the next room.

A late breakfast is ready. In the backyard freshly smeared with cow dung, a sumptuous poha is polished off in minutes. A few red-whiskered bulbuls interrupt the coppersmith. Another round of tea follows. Late guests, a Pune family, check in for the weekend. Their healthy boy tests the robust swing by the portico. Finally, conversation slips beyond pleasantries.

'What do you do in Velas if the eggs don't hatch?'

'Between the two rounds of the beach, what do you do anyway all day?'

The answer, of course, is very little. Or is it?

🦂

A Mumbai family brought its own turtle story to the beach on Saturday evening. By the time we spotted the commotion by the breakers, they had forced their pet, a soft-shelled turtle that is a sweet-water species, into the sea. A sizeable crowd of unsuspecting tourists cheered on.

Back at the homestay, the Mumbai gang mourned 'the murder' well past dinnertime. On the beach next morning, they chanced upon the creature that had managed to scamper out of the salt water in time and escape predators by sliding under weeds. The SNM staff would soon return the softy to a pond. The 'famous four', as they called themselves, had their souvenir anecdote.

Sea turtles need secure stretches of sand above the shoreline for laying eggs. At Velas, olive ridleys use just about 2 kilometres where the waves do not break too close to the rocky hills or the weeds have not hardened the sand with their roots. For a virgin beach, it is dirty. Much of the garbage dumped along the region's busy tourist beaches washes up here due to mischievous tidal currents. A cliff running somewhere under the breakers discourages swimming. A casuarina plantation runs parallel to the sea. The sand is black, the rocks porous, wind-beaten, with a smattering of dead barnacles.

In the south, a decaying hillock juts out to the sea. Its lower mounds drown during high tide. When the water recedes, sea creatures get caught in small crater-like holes in the rock. To spot action, make sure your shadow does not startle them as you lean over to peep. My luck ran out with a few tiny fish and crabs but locals have spotted even octopuses in those natural receptacles.

In the north, just above the shoreline, the sand slopes up steeply, too steep in places for any turtle to climb and nest. Where the casuarina plantation ends, the beach is cut up by a narrow creek beyond which the sea catches up with the road that links Velas to Bankot and the world beyond. During low tide, one can walk along the breakers all the way to Bankot where the Savitri river joins the sea.

Typical of Konkan, rows of hillocks stand guard by the beach. These forested heights and the surrounding plantations can keep any birdwatcher happy. Hornbills gave us a miss. But within our first few hours at the beach, Sandesh clicked a White-bellied sea eagle in flight with a sea krait dangling from its talons. Walking alongside, local school teacher and SNM staff, Mohan Upadhye, confirmed that the majestic birds were frequent fliers in these skies.

A White-bellied sea eagle usually pairs by the age of six and uses the same nest, unless disturbed, for the rest of its twenty-five to thirty-year-long life. Soon, we followed Mohan to an ancient mango tree in a village courtyard. In a corner of its lofty crown was a large, clumsy arrangement of twigs. The white-bellied couple, long-time neighbours on the ground informed us, could be spotted around the nest at dawn and dusk. Greedy Sandesh wished there was a chick. Of course, there was, he was assured, and quite a 'big' one. As if on cue, the adolescent announced itself with a shrill goose call.

2

Unlike most Konkan villages, Velas sends no fishing boats to the sea. Its predominantly Hindu population depends on mango and other plantations for a living. The nearest hub of the Kolis, the fishing community, is a short drive away at Bankot where, every morning, dozens of colourful, tiny fishing boats dot the estuary of the Savitri river. By the jetties, lively music plays out in stalls selling tea and snacks, satiated cats lurk with a cultivated indifference, children pose and their mothers dote on them distractedly, waiting for the day's catch.

Close to Bankot, Himmat Garh or Fort Victoria is a few hundred metres' climb from the blacktop road. Atop this robust sixteenth century naval structure now in ruins, the view of the horizon is complete—with the hills, the sea and the estuary. A little downhill in the south are the abandoned graves of an Englishman's wife and daughter, drowned in a shipwreck in the Savitri river nearly 150 years ago.

At Velas, the nights rush you to sleep. After the evening film show at the SNM office, there is not much to do. Unless you drive a few kilometres north under the moon, settle down where, right on the beach by the road, a forward watch-post of Himmat Garh stands in ruins, and curse the distracting lights on the other side of the estuary.

Alternatively, you could stock your host's kitchen during the day with the freshest of pomfret and prawns from Bankot and work the gastric juices late into the night. Three statutory warnings though:

- Stick to fries if your cook is a vegetarian (though Velas has a killer recipe for prawns).
- Beware of Koli saleswomen. We faced a vivacious Devni and forgot all about bargaining.
- Ask discreetly if you want to try a village tipple derived from coconut that goes devilishly well with seafood.

☙

Walking to the beach through a patch of mangroves on our fourth evening, I meet an elderly couple from Pune. Sriram tells me that he and wife, Sulabha, were at Velas on the same day the previous year and watched a handful of hatchlings walk. Maybe, there will be an encore on the anniversary.

We are on the beach. Volunteers go through the routine. It is all quiet under the baskets. A journalist from the Marathi press chats up with the volunteers. In the horizon, I see Anna walking briskly towards us.

Gopinath Ganpat Mahadik, aka Anna, a villager in his mid-sixties, is the face of turtle conservation at Velas. Anna has been guarding the SNM hatchery since it was set up in 2002, scanning the beach for new nests and guiding the volunteers.

From a distance, Anna summons Mohan, who rushes with a basket in hand. Minutes later, we see them poking the sand with a stick a couple of hundred metres away. Then Mohan starts digging. By the time we run up to them, half of the treasure is already in the basket.

In the next half hour, the eggs are placed in a new nest inside the hatchery. Covered in sand up to his elbows, Mohan is happy. 'We were getting impatient for the hatchlings and now we've got more eggs to hatch. But trust Anna to spot the faintest of turtle trails and sniff out a nest.'

Gopinath is standing away, scanning the sky. Those calm, probing eyes and the deep furrows across his sunburnt face could well belong to an ancient mariner. The only time I spoke to him in broken Marathi, Gopinath told me he was a farmer with some land nearby. This time, I seek the Marathi journalist's help to decode his grunts.

Gopinath's family of seven includes two grandsons. He remembers the days when villagers used to raid turtle nests and sell the eggs for Rs 2 each. There was no taker for turtle eggs in Velas but the loot was in demand among the Kolis in Bankot. But things have changed in the past ten years. Now not a single egg is stolen.

I quickly do the maths. At hundred eggs per nest, even hundred nests would fetch just Rs 20,000. Last year, homestays alone earned Velas more than Rs 2 lakh. Surely, conservation has won the bet here.

Gopinath says the village elders recommended him to the turtle NGO because he stayed close to the beach. Of course, it helped that he could feel the wind, read the position of the moon and tell when turtles would be visiting the beach. I wonder how Gopinath knows so much about turtles. Was he one of the nest raiders a long time ago? The journalist hesitates. It is getting dark, he says.

Back at the homestay, the elderly host breaks off from the TV to console us. Spotting a nest is far rarer than watching eggs hatch, he says. We were lucky that, for once, Gopinath was late because the NGO team always recovered eggs with no outsiders around. After all, he explains, eggs used to be stolen until a few years ago. I agree, then push my luck.

Of course, our host has known Gopinath all his life. So how does Gopinath know all about turtles? 'How else?' the old man chuckles, warmly, before returning to his TV. It is time for us to pack up. But then, a change of heart is in order at Velas.

Wild Dogs

KRUPAKAR AND SENANI

It's November. The dark monsoon clouds that unified the earth and the sky into one undistinguishable whole during the last four months have retreated. It is time for our wild dogs to find a suitable place to give birth to their pups, which means that tough times lay ahead of us. Tracking them on foot is a treacherous task, not only because of their secretive ways during denning and the terrain that they traverse but also because this is the time that the ticks breed too! Our only consolation is the thought of a pleasurable hot bath at the end of the day.

It is almost fifteen years since we have been on the trail of the dhole in the Nilgiri Biosphere Reserve in southern India. We have been conversing with several generations of these wild dogs—their behaviour in different situations, the areas they prefer in various seasons, the dogs that are likely to leave the pack in a certain year and those likely to follow the dog that takes the lead, their forest routes, their secret resting places—they are all very familiar to us.

Then again, every time we speak in this manner with any confidence, they decide to remind us that they are magically elusive.

We haven't seen them for the last ten days. We are feeling terribly helpless again. All our predictions, and the knowledge and skills we have acquired over the years following the dhole have deserted us without notice.

This is not new to us though. Every time we meet, they throw a few new questions at us and vanish into thin air; and then we get back to the basics and spend days reading scientific papers on the African wild dog and discussing social animal behaviour with scientists. Back in the field, when we do find them, they surprise us again by posing a whole new set of questions.

Asiatic wild dogs or dhole are pack-living social animals. The alpha male and female play the lead role. They are the only ones to breed in a pack, while others work for the common good of the pack. The hierarchy is strict and they fiercely defend their territory. But if you want to know anything beyond this, the path gets confusing and murky and eventually you get totally lost.

The trail of the dhole always runs this course. The more time you spend seeking answers, the more questions they pose.

The alpha female that we are presently following is Kennai. Her parents were from the adjacent Mudumalai forests. Kennai left her natal pack when her mother was killed by a tiger and an unrelated female took over as the alpha female of the pack. She was no more than about one-and-a-half years old then. She pursued her dream of forming her own pack under very difficult circumstances. Surviving in these forests as a lone dhole is an absolute rarity.

Her story continued like a long-drawn epic drama, with unexpected twists and turns and numerous sub-plots, as she went on taking extraordinary risks, often endangering her life. And, as for us, we jumped onto this epic journey like mute spectators, often losing track of our own lives. Sometimes banner headlines in the newspaper, like the death of a chief minister in a helicopter crash, would reach us a month later!

Fifteen years have slipped by unnoticed, following these dogs.

But the dhole can still surprise us at will. And they have done it again and have vanished for the past ten days. We know well where to look for them, and what signs would lead us to them…or so we thought. This time it seems as if our days of logical searching are over and we are on a real wild goose chase.

You lose track in the tall grass or in the bushes and that is when the ticks get the better of you. We have been talking to everyone about the ecosystem, so the last thing we should be doing is denying the ticks the blood they need to breed! With no escape in sight, we accept them, and soon we don't even notice that we are scratching ourselves indecently in public.

On one such trying day, we ended our search in the forest and started towards a nearby village to find some transport back to the camp. We were walking along the ridge of the hillock on the fringes of the forest, from where we could see the village and a tribal hamlet. We suddenly heard a sound so familiar and so musical to our ears. It was the begging call of a sub-adult dhole.

Early next morning we were back. By evening, we were sure that the den was on the same hillock—but why so close to the tribal hamlet, of all places? We were puzzled.

Rather than looking for reasons, our immediate priority was to see that no one goes near the den. We were quite sure that Kennai would vacate the area and vanish again if any human even accidentally strayed near it. Already exhausted, we were definitely not up for another long search.

The only way out would be to keep a constant vigil on the den from a distance so that we could stop any villager from going too close to it. That was no easy job. One has to sit alone without being noticed from six in the morning till six in the evening, doing absolutely nothing in a degraded jungle, keeping our eyes fixed in the direction of the den for any slight movement. It is a sort of meditation that needs special genetic material to sustain. To be honest, it can be absolutely boring!

We wondered who would have that kind of a DNA. Not a city slicker, for sure. Four years ago, we had put a young enthusiastic naturalist from Bengaluru, who had expressed an extreme passion for wildlife, on a similar job. When he first arrived, he looked quite impressive in his camouflage clothes, a hat to match and a pair of expensive binoculars. At that time it was our policy not to discourage youngsters...after all, they are our future hope for conservation.

But that boy had proved to be a disaster. We had discussed the plan in detail with him and had instructed him on how to sit in one place and observe the dogs from a distance. In an effort to enthuse him, we had described colourfully how the forest unveils itself after an hour or so to the quiet observer. But he had done quite the opposite, he had done a demonstrative 'march past' with his noisy shoes and fancy hat in front of the den, probably hoping to grab the attention of the dogs, and attract them! By the time we realized it, the dogs had abandoned the den.

Even our well-trained and dedicated trackers from the nearby village would not be reliable enough when it came to such jobs. They are too young and hyperactive to sit tight in one place for so long.

When we scanned our memories, the name that stood out was Mada from the Betta Kurumba tribe. Mada is an old acquaintance. With a miniskirt-like lungi wrapped around his waist and a machete which was like the extension of his right hand, Mada would suddenly appear on a forest track where we were on the trail of the dhole. He would hardly talk or even smile. Sometimes he would utter a word or two about the dhole. In a few minutes, he would have disappeared into the forest just as suddenly as he had appeared. One thing was certain: he would never be spotted by someone if he did not want to be seen; and if he was ever asked about wild dogs by a stranger, his answer would always be that he had never ever seen a dhole in his entire life!

Somehow we knew that Mada was the right person for this job. There is no glamour or adventure in the business of observing the dhole from a distance of more than a kilometre, especially because one gets to see them only once or twice a day, slipping through the bushes like shadows.

When we approached Mada's hamlet, we first met Kyatha, who we know well. On enquiring about Mada, he asked: 'Which Mada Sir?'

What did he mean by that? Wasn't he behaving exactly like a man from the city, not knowing his own neighbours, particularly when the neighbourhood was a cluster of no more than ten huts?

He went on: 'There are seven Madas in this hamlet. Which one do you want, saa?'

The tribals are simple people, we knew. But so many Madas in a hamlet of ten huts was difficult to accept. As we were debating how to identify 'our' Mada, the man himself appeared from nowhere as usual.

'Mada, what is your name?' was our first question. 'Nadu Mada saa,' he said. 'Nadu' means the middle one. They obviously had their own way of telling the many Madas apart!

We came straight to the point.

'Mada, are you working anywhere now?'

'Yes, saa...'

'Where?'

'Hotellu, saa...'

As we did not want him to leave his job in a hotel for the short-term job we were offering, we were in a dilemma.

Mada broke the silence with, 'What can I do for you, saa...?'

We explained, and asked if he could suggest someone like him.

'I will come, saa...' Mada said without a second thought.

'But you are already working in the hotel.'

'That is okay, saa... They pay Rs 30 whenever I go for work, saa...'

We knew that he would any day prefer working in the forest than in a hotel.

Though the days were still warm, the mornings and evenings were quite cool for Mada to work. He did not need too many instructions about his job, except for things like how and when he would have to contact us. We were quite happy that we could get Mada to help us at the right time, since we had other things to follow up during the next few days.

The next day we spotted Mada at a tea shop in the village close to where Kennai had her den. He was smartly dressed. Though he is used to his short lungi, we had given him trousers and shirts, as it would be cold when he left for the forest early in the morning. We had also fixed a wage of Rs 150 per day and had paid him Rs 500 in advance. We felt badly let down, as he was not supposed to leave his sentry post near the den for the whole day.

We stopped to enquire. Mada took some time to raise his head. When he looked up, he said after a long pause, 'Trouballu, saa...'

It was thoughtless, probably stupid, on our part to employ a tribal to watch over the den as villagers—who believe they are higher up in the social hierarchy—dominate over these simple people. Mada would never be able to stop them from going near the den. A villager would have challenged Mada and perhaps scared away the dogs too. Kennai must have shifted her den by now. These dogs are extremely shy when it comes to denning and they have good reason to be wary of humans...

When the British first arrived in India, they branded the dhole as vermin—the dogs allegedly decimated the game animals that the British wanted to kill! The dhole were slaughtered mercilessly. In fact, they carried a bounty on their heads until the late twentieth century. Even Indian wildlife managers thought they were threatening the deer population and thereby, the survival of the tiger. The dhole were seen as 'bloody killers' for the way in which they bring down their prey. Few people saw the leopard and the tiger kill since they are nocturnal hunters. The dhole, on the other hand, are twilight hunters. Unlike the tiger or leopard, the dhole is too small to deliver the killing bite. They are forced to use their numbers. They bite at their prey and it dies by loss of blood and shock. But death is death. In fact, the time taken by big cats to kill prey bigger than themselves is usually longer than the time taken by the dhole.

But villainous characteristics were attributed to the dhole. The fact that they had evolved over millions of years in these forests meant nothing to their persecutors. They were poisoned and shot in large numbers. As though that was not enough, given a chance, the people in and around dhole habitats have always stolen their hard-earned meal.

All this has made wild dogs extremely wary of human presence, especially during denning and when the pups are small and vulnerable. Thankfully, they are now protected by law.

Aware of this history, we were sure that we had made a terrible mistake by engaging Mada to guard the den; one of us should have kept vigil.

Expecting the inevitable answer, with a heavy heart we asked:

'What trouble, Mada?'

'*Beedi* trouballu, saa... I have run out of *beedis*, saa...'

Three days later, on hearing no news from Mada, we went to check. We scanned the area and whistled. No reply... Mada was not familiar with our forest signals as he was new to the team. So we decided to try and track him down like we track a wild animal.

After a while we found a bed of *Butea* leaves under a naayi beete (common name) tree. It looked like Mada had slept there that morning. A little further, we found a *Butea* leaf with some left-over rice morsels. Mada was around for sure. We were struggling to find other clues, when suddenly, from nowhere, Mada appeared right behind us.

We were quite happy.

'Hey Mada, are the dogs still there?'

'Yes, saa...'

'Did you see them?'

'Yes, saa... The mom and children came down the hillock, saa...' he addressed the dhole like his own family.

'When did they come down, Mada?'

'It was when I was eating rice, saa...'

'What time were you eating rice, Mada?'

'...That was when the Jakkalli bus went by, saa...' Two kilometres away was a village road on which a bus would pass twice or thrice a day. Mada could hear the bus from where he was sitting.

This has always been our problem. Whenever we sit down to write a serious academic article about the dhole and a new scientific finding about them, we end up telling a story that sounds totally unrelated! And if we say that it is important to know the village bus timings to study the dhole, we would sound ridiculous, wouldn't we?

We honestly try to stay focused on our goal and be very objective in our observations. But both the dhole and the tribals are so elusive and peculiar in their own ways that it is impossible to understand them without putting ourselves in their shoes.

Still the study of the dhole goes on and we do find something new along the way every now and then. This time our pack has come surprisingly close to the village. The same dogs which were always running away from humans, have now run into humans. Strange? Yes, but we had come across this behaviour earlier too. Many years of experience and data have shown us that in areas where tiger density is high, dhole have often adopted this strategy.

Our guess is that the tigers roam less in areas where human activity is high. Taking advantage of this situation, Kennai has chosen a den close to a tribal settlement to avoid tigers when the pups are still defenceless little creatures. What other reason could have driven this mom-to-be to deliver in a neighbourhood she loved to avoid?

Kennai is a survivor. Nature has taught her bitter lessons and she has used cleverness, guile and, sometimes, diplomacy to live, struggle and fight another day. Come to think of it, our struggles at understanding the dhole are linked to Kennai's travails. Both Kennai and us probably struggled and learnt many a nature's lesson together, each but in different degrees. She, undoubtedly, was the better pupil. For, it was she who opened for us a new window to nature.

Warm Turtle in Cold Waters: The Leatherback's Journey

KARTIK SHANKER

Looking for luth

In the late 1980s, I became fascinated with sea turtles through a student conservation programme that we had started in Chennai on the east coast of India. Each night during the nesting season, a group of college students would trudge along the coast looking for olive ridley turtle nests and relocate them to a hatchery. Olive ridley turtles are the smallest sea turtles with a carapace length of about 2 feet and weigh about 50 kilograms. Leatherback turtles are the largest, with a carapace length of about 5 feet, and weigh over 500 kilograms. These turtles have long been known as champion transoceanic travellers, migrating thousands of kilometres between nesting and feeding grounds, and are also extraordinary divers, going down 1000 metres or more in search of jellyfish. To a sea turtle neophyte, such a creature was the stuff of legend.

More than a decade after I first heard about leatherback turtles, I found myself on a ship from Port Blair to Campbell Bay, the port on Great Nicobar Island. I was heading out to the field camp at

Galathea Bay on the south-eastern coast of the island. My partner, Meera, who was going to conduct a field study on the endemic Nicobar tree shrew, and I were to join the field assistants of the Andaman and Nicobar Environmental Team (ANET). Saw Glen and Saw Agu had established a camp at Galathea beach, at the mouth of the Galathea river, about 41 kilometres from Campbell Bay and about 11 kilometres from the lighthouse at the southern tip of the island. Arriving in Campbell Bay, our first challenge was to find provisions, especially vegetables, which disappeared rapidly from the market after the ship's arrival, and to find transport to Galathea. Fortunately for us, autorickshaws had just found their way to the Great Nicobar Island, and one of the two autos agreed to take us to our destination.

Travelling a distance of 35 kilometres, we saw a store that was called 'the southern-most grocery store in India'. A little way past, we arrived at our camp—a clearing with a few huts, nestled in a coastal forest that would be devastated by the tsunami some years later. Our biggest worry was the saltwater crocodile that we were asked to watch out for, if we ventured too close to the river. We needed no warnings; on the beach, a dead leatherback lay decaying, decapitated by a hungry 'salty'.

That night, we wandered for several hours hearing the waves beating down on the narrow Galathea beach, less than a metre wide in parts. A decade of waiting stretched a few more hours of peering into the breakers, listening for the flapping of giant flippers, until finally, we saw the luth, as she is known in some parts of the world. Ungainly, clumsy, belaboured breaths, sighs of exhaustion, she lay like a beached whale, but one with a purpose. She dragged her 6-feet-long frame on the beach with her elegantly shaped front flippers. She was single-minded in her task of digging a nest, with her hind flipper flapping like an elephant's ear as she scooped out sand. After digging an enormous body pit, she created a nest over

2 feet deep and deposited about 100 eggs in it. Then she covered her nest and spent the better part of an hour throwing sand around, camouflaging her nest, in effect, creating a crater on the beach that we would have the misfortune of falling into several times. When she returned, the horizon was bright, and the chromatic three-dimensional view of her was even more spectacular. We followed her to the waves, which she lumbered and laboured towards, but once in the swell, she disappeared like an apparition that had never been.

A smattering of surveys and science

The very first sea turtle survey of Great Nicobar Island was carried out as far back as 1979. The Madras Crocodile Bank Trust (MCBT) had a few years earlier discovered that Satish Bhaskar, an erstwhile student of the Indian Institute of Technology, had an appetite for adventure and a passion for sea turtles. Satish had already completed the first ever surveys of Kutch, Gujarat and the Lakshadweep Islands. An extensive survey of the Andaman and Nicobar Islands followed in 1978–79. During this trip, Satish visited the Great Nicobar Island and located the Galathea beach on the east coast, discovering a major leatherback nesting site there.

The beach was not surveyed again till Manjula Tiwari, a budding ecologist from Pondicherry (now Puducherry), visited in the early 1990s, confirming the importance of this nesting beach. Manjula revisited the Nicobars with Satish and their surveys indicated that a large number of leatherback turtles nested at Galathea and several beaches on the west coast of Great Nicobar. Subsequently, Manish Chandi, while working on aspects of human ecology, documented nesting beaches on Little Nicobar Island as well.

The first monitoring programme was established in 2000 by Harry Andrews of the MCBT through a Government of India–UNDP funded project. The project conducted the first complete season of monitoring Galathea beach, including the tagging of adult turtles using Passive Integrated Transponders (PIT) tags. PIT tags are injected into the animal and are read by using a scanner; these work better than conventional metal tags for leatherback turtles. Shreyas Krishnan, who worked as a researcher on the project, spent nearly eight months at Galathea, helping identify the peak nesting season, which is from November to March.

A year later, Meera and I spent a season at the beach, monitoring and tagging turtles with ANET, and collecting tissue samples for my genetics project through the Wildlife Institute of India. We also visited the west coast and found high densities of leatherbacks nesting at Kophen Heat beach. Over 150 turtles were tagged each year during 2000–02 and close to 500 nests recorded for each season at this beach alone. During the peak season, ten or more turtles would come ashore to nest on a single night.

Monitoring continued for another couple of years at this site till the December 2004 tsunami, which devastated the islands. The beach at Galathea and its surrounding forests were completely destroyed, and Ambika Tripathy, MCBT's researcher and several visiting researchers died tragically. Saw Agu survived, however, enduring more than ten days at sea on a log.*

A survey by Naveen Namboothri, a postdoctoral researcher at the Indian Institute of Science, and Saw Agu indicates that the beaches have formed again on the southern side of the Galathea river, and that several hundred turtles nested there during the 2010–11 season.

Almost mammal

Leatherback turtles are the largest living reptiles. Huge and lumbering as they are on land, their languid grace in the water is a remarkable contrast. They have beautifully streamlined bodies, long powerful

---

* For the astonishing tale of survival, see URL: http://madrascrocbank. blogspot.in/2007/12/surviving-tsunami-at-galathea-bridge.html

fore flippers, and a physiology that frequently defies biological wisdom. They have also been recorded diving to depths below 1000 metres, which no other air-breathing vertebrate apart from sperm whales can do. They migrate thousands of kilometres from tropical beaches to cold temperate waters and wander in the world's oceans in search of food. Like other sea turtles, leatherbacks use the earth's magnetic field to navigate between feeding grounds and breeding grounds, and are believed to return to their natal beaches (where they were born) to nest as adults.

Sea turtles, though remarkably adapted for marine life, are still tied to the land for the most important aspect of their lives, namely reproduction. This is one of the constraints in their adaptation to the aquatic environment, that they still have to be able to move and nest on land, often several times in a season. These turtles nest only once in two or three years, but may nest six or more times in the same season. It is also a stage of their lifecycle when they are most vulnerable, both adults as well as eggs and hatchlings.

Reptiles have generally been described as sluggish, cold-blooded ectotherms. This stereotype has been demolished by leatherbacks. These animals have been known to maintain their body temperatures 18 degree Celsius above the ambient temperature, which allows them to foray into the cold temperate waters of the northern Atlantic and Pacific oceans, and also to forage for jellyfish in the deep sea. They are believed to regulate their body temperature by a combination of their large size, insulation and a blood circulation mechanism, known as a counter-current heat-exchanger, found at the junction of the flippers and the body. This mode of thermoregulation, that can neither be classified as homeothermy (as in birds or mammals) or poikilothermy (as in fish, amphibians and most reptiles), has been named as gigantothermy. These animals provide important clues to the evolution of traits thus far believed to be the exclusive domain of birds and mammals. They also provide hints about dinosaur life, such as, where they could have lived, their physiology and metabolism.

Learning about leatherbacks

Apart from surveys, little research has been carried out on leatherback turtles on the islands. In the mid-1990s, Arjun Sivasundar carried out a research project on the nest site selection of leatherback turtles on the Little Andaman Island. In the early 2000s, we initiated genetic studies on the leatherbacks of the Great Nicobar Island. In May 2007, Manish Chandi and I visited Little Andaman Island to explore the establishment of a long-term monitoring site for leatherback turtles. Our visit to South Bay was uneventful, but on West Bay, we got stranded on the beach as the boat was unable to get close enough to the shore for us to get back on. This resulted in a twelve-hour trek over uplifted rocks and coral (from the earthquake), waist-high Ipomoea and marshy grasslands.

Following the survey, we established a camp in South Bay in January 2008, as a collaboration between the Indian Institute of Science (IISc), Dakshin Foundation, and ANET. The research at Little Andaman includes monitoring of nests, predation, monitoring of nest temperatures, collection of tissues for genetic analysis and tagging. Since the sex of a sea turtle hatchling is determined by incubation temperature, climate change could have potential impacts on sex ratios. Hence, monitoring of temperatures, along with the sexing of hatchings, could provide critical insights about the impact of global climate change on these populations. Similarly, it is important to determine the relationship of these leatherback populations with those in other ocean basins, but also at a finer scale of resolution, with those in the Nicobars and other parts of the Indian Ocean.

Most recently, we have initiated satellite telemetry studies to track the movements of these turtles. Satellite transmitters or Platform Transmitter Terminals (PTTs) send signals that are received by polar orbiting satellites, which in turn are used to determine their location. In November 2010, Adhith Swaminathan, a field researcher from IISc, and the ANET field team established camps at both South Bay and West Bay on Little Andaman Island. In January 2011, Naveen and I joined Adhith at the West Bay camp and fitted three transmitters on leatherback turtles for the first time in India. Of the seven turtles that were tagged in 2011 and 2012, two turtles transmitted for about six months. Four out of six turtles travelled south-east of the Andaman and Nicobar Islands, two along the coast of Sumatra and two beyond Cocos (Keeling) Island, towards Western Australia. Two turtles moved south-west of the islands, one of which travelled south of the British Ocean Territory. Turtle 103333, tagged on 4 January 2011, transmitted for 179 days and travelled the longest distance of 7,312 kilometres (a straight line distance of 4,185 kilometres). Several more turtles have been tagged since then, and some have ranged as far east as Western Australia and as far west as Madagascar and Mozambique.

Saving sea turtles

In addition to natural predators, human-related problems such as exploitation of eggs, depredation of nests by feral predators, erosion and consumption of adults for meat have depleted many sea turtle populations around the world. Fortunately for leatherbacks, adults are not eaten in most parts of the world. However, egg exploitation remains a major threat. There is predation of eggs by wild boar, monitor lizards and feral dogs throughout the islands.

Since leatherbacks and olive ridleys nest near river mouths, many of their nesting beaches are dynamic and change from year to year. This is, in fact, a natural phenomenon. However, in many parts of India (as of the world), this has been aggravated by human activities such as sand-mining. Other major problems are anti-erosion measures such as the construction of sea walls. Much of Kerala and Lakshadweep has been walled by granite to prevent the erosion of developed land. Most often, this has simply led to the erosion of beaches elsewhere, often those used by turtles. This has already lead to the loss of nesting habitats in some parts of the Andaman Islands, and the situation will aggravate with increasing human development and activity.

Leatherback populations are believed to have declined sharply from near a 100,000 to less than 10,000 in the Pacific. While many populations in the Atlantic are stable or increasing, there is a need to monitor and safeguard critical populations in the Indian Ocean. In the Andaman and Nicobar Islands, many beaches are currently protected because of their remoteness, and the lack of infrastructure and development in many islands, particularly in the Nicobars, even more so after the 2004 tsunami. However, the increase in fishing pressures and the introduction of methods such as long-lining could impact the leatherback adults.

Much remains to be learned about these extraordinary animals. Researchers around the world are studying various aspects of their biology. At the same time, conservationists are working overtime to safeguard their populations through a range of measures that include instituting community monitoring and conservation projects, hatchery and beach monitoring programmes to protect the eggs and influencing fishery-related policy to lessen the impact on adults. Working with leatherback turtles has and will always be challenging, but deeply rewarding as well. Leatherbacks are larger than life, a symbol of the wonder of biological adaptation, an inspiration for those who spend their time discovering their secrets and a flagship for the conservation of sea turtles and their many habitats.

My First Days in the Field

The path I followed reached a little stream. A log thrown across the stream served as a bridge, and the drop to the stream bed, covered with pointy rocks, was high enough to frighten. It curved left upwards and cut diagonally across the hill face. After fifteen minutes it looped around the hillside, which was steep on both sides. Massive trees bordered the path. The fog had thickened and made it difficult to see beyond a few metres. This was my first time alone in a rainforest and I did not like it one bit.

Suddenly, a great grey shape loomed out of the mist in front of me, trumpeting. I leapt off the path, lost my footing and went stumbling and lurching down the slope. To my shock, the grey shape rapidly resolved itself into an elephant. The giant animal jogged off past me in the opposite direction. An adrenalin rush like I'd never experienced before hit me. I sat huddled for an hour till I was sure that the elephant had gone and then gingerly retraced my steps, peeping around every corner. After what seemed like an eternity, I reached the Sengaltheri forest resthouse—the place that was supposed to be my home for the next couple of years. I decided that this life filled with nasty brutish animals was not for me. I would pack my bags, go back to Bombay and get a degree in business management.

Initial days at Sengaltheri

The day before had been traumatic. John Oates, my field supervisor, had dropped me at the bottom of the hill as the road up to the resthouse had been washed away by the rains. We found a road crew to carry my stuff up to the resthouse after wading through a stream. At the resthouse a boy had been employed to cook for me. In the absence of a shared language, we communicated through gestures. The rain made it difficult to light a fire. For the better part of the night, I kept shifting from one end of the room to another, to avoid the rain water that dribbled through the roof. There was no way that I could get much sleep there.

I woke up the next morning to a thick blanket of fog. I had come here to study monkeys and found the elephant instead.

When I got back to Sengaltheri, the cook managed to convey, using a crude sign language, that the stream below the resthouse, which we had crossed the evening before, had flooded. We were cut off, and I couldn't run away immediately to pursue a business degree. We were cut off for five days, and I used these days to get used to the forest. And found myself loving it!

I did find bonnet monkeys in the vicinity. Since the resthouse wasn't comfortable, I spent most of my time exploring the area around it. I soon discovered the vistas Sengaltheri is renowned for (among the few persons who have been able to visit it), and was transfixed by them. The monkeys were fun to watch, even though they were very shy. Steaming elephant dung continued to horrify me for a while, though, I even got used to this.

On the fifth day, after we were cut off, a couple of John's assistants made it to Sengaltheri; John had very thoughtfully sent a packet of cigarettes with them. But by this time I did not want to leave.

When the rain stopped, I walked down to Kalakkad town from Sengaltheri. Having walked three hours downhill, we reached the town full of people, cows and buses. Sengaltheri was definitely better.

An elderly gentleman came running out of a house situated on the border of the town and asked, 'Excuse me sir, are you a central government official studying the lifestyles of people of Tirunelveli district?' I burst out laughing. He walked off in a huff.

Then it was back to Kakachi, on a nearby tea estate, and John Oates. I was supposed to take charge of the jeep when he left. At this time he realized that I did not know how to drive a car. The first driving lesson lasted fifteen minutes. A thoroughly rattled John then got off saying it was too dangerous to sit in the car while I was learning, especially on the treacherous mountain roads. I practised on my own, driving round the little golf course in the tea estate. As there was no traffic, even if I drove off the road, there were no chances of accidents and injury. So I survived and learned—rather fast.

After a few days John and I went to the plains again—this time to another part of the sanctuary, the Mundanthurai plateau. In order to get there, we had to cross the town of Vikramasingapuram. It was one of the most congested towns in the area and every time we drove through, we wondered how we had passed it unscathed. However, the denizens of South Indian villages appear to melt away magically as vehicles approach. The road suddenly burst out of the town into an expanse of rice fields, went across a river and suddenly the hills began. The entrance to the sanctuary was at the base of the hills and here onwards, the road climbed uphill, overlooking the town and the fields surrounding it. It then went through a cleft in the hills to enter a bowl-shaped valley, through which the Tambraparni river flowed.

At the other end of the valley, there were four enormous silver-coloured pipes going down the hillside, into a building at the bottom of the valley. This was the power generation house for the Lower

Tambraparni Dam, built in 1935. Next to the pipes was a large sheet of rocks that meandered down the hillside. It was the remains of a magnificent waterfall that existed before the dam was built, and I was once fortunate enough to see it in full flow during a cyclone.

The road skirted the valley and after a series of sharp turns, crossed the pipes, went through another cleft and reached the village of Papanasam Lower Dam, which later became my base for the next few years. It then passed through another cleft to cross a low range of hills and entered a plateau. The scrub forest vegetation of the hills now gave way to larger trees, many of which had been replaced with teak plantations. Over the next few kilometres we saw a few spotted deer. We crossed a bridge and stopped at a magnificent two-storey structure by the riverside. This was the Mundanthurai Forest Resthouse.

The building was constructed in 1892 and had been renovated in the 1930s to convert its single bedroom to two. There was one large room both upstairs and downstairs with a verandah surrounding three sides. On one end of the verandah was a bathroom and on the other a spare room, which doubled as a sleeping accommodation. I was given the room downstairs, which was my home for the next year and a half. Nearby, there were a lot of dilapidated structures, two of which, located a couple of hundred metres away, were occupied by the local forest staff. The remaining were deserted. Although there were a number of persons posted here, they were only to be seen, and in their uniforms too, when some senior functionary paid a visit.

On my first evening out, a local boy—the son of a forest guard—accompanied me. He spoke a little English which made conversation possible. I was flooded with a barrage of questions about my work. What was so special about these monkeys? They were the same as other monkeys anywhere. So what if they lived in the forest? Isn't that what monkeys were supposed to do? Of course, the males were bigger than the females; that was the natural order of things. He listened to me keenly and then the questions became more critical. He started making astute remarks about the happenings in the group. I realized that I had found my assistant who would help me with the research at Mundanthurai. This was Narayanaraj (later referred to as Narayana), who went on to become a wildlife biologist himself. He has since acquired two Master's degrees and a teaching fellowship at the Harvard University, and has also worked at the Audobon Society.

My research was on bonnet monkeys, one of the commonest monkeys in southern India. They are the nasty little brats that walk up to you on the road, snatch food from your hand and threaten you with ugly faces if you have the temerity to object. Tracing the river upwards from Mundanthurai, I found a group of bonnet monkeys that seemed uninfluenced by humanity. Initially, they wouldn't let me approach; but soon the little ones would come and peer at me. The adults took a bit longer to warm up to me. With the exception of one old female, whose tail was missing, they all treated me as part of the landscape. They would run away at the sight of other humans except for Narayana, whom they would see bring me eatables that some of them associated with food. As the days passed they allowed me to come closer, and closer.

The group had fourteen animals in it. There were two males, including a crotchety one well past his prime. There were two sub-adult males, both constantly straying from the group. Occasionally, they would carry infants around—a strange trait for a male monkey. There were four females, all with very different personalities. One was old and bad-tempered. Another would constantly forget her infant and leave him behind at awkward places, to be retrieved usually by one of the young males. Then there was a variety of juveniles of various sizes.

I developed Sengaltheri as the second field site. The resthouse was leaky and dilapidated, but the view it offered was out of this world. One could gaze at the forest from a height of around 1,000 metres leading down to the plains and across them to the sea about 50 kilometres away. The lighthouse at Tuticorin and the harbour there could be seen every night. Once I had settled down in the resthouse and made it barely liveable, the forest department woke up to the fact that the resthouse could actually be used and that the location was fantastic. However, the resthouse was uninhabitable by any civilized norms: it had a leaky roof, no bathrooms, no kitchen and no furniture apart from a string cot with broken strings. So they decided to rebuild it and I had to move out and live in a tent in the resthouse yard. At the same time, the road uphill was extended all the way to the resthouse. The plan then was to take the road right through the rainforest and link it up with the road going into the tea estate, which would have meant destroying a swathe of rain forest 8 kilometres long. Luckily, good sense prevailed in this case.

Around this time, I had my second elephant experience. One night I heard a noise outside the tent. I opened the flap of the tent and peered out. Lo and behold! A dark shape stood looming over the tent, producing loud sniffling noises. Jumbo was sniffing away at the tent. There was no place to run, and even if there had been a place, there was no way I could have outrun the animal. Terror took over me as I pulled the blanket to cover my head, and lay there shivering. After a couple of minutes, which seemed like hours to me, he must have decided that he had spread enough alarm and despondency and therefore, went away. I wasn't very comfortable in that tent anymore, but there was a decided lack of choices at the time.

Thirty-five years later

Apart from these wildlife episodes, what was it like being a biologist thirty-five years back? It might be instructive to look at what has changed, and what has not.

There has been a sea change in the attitude of the forest department. In 1976, all the concerned authorities I had to deal with thought I was certifiably insane. Research on wildlife was unheard of those days, except in a couple of places like the Bombay Natural History Society, which had established bird-ringing camps.

Back then the ranger was God. He controlled your life, including whether you could see his bosses or not. Poaching, grazing and firewood collection was rampant, and complaining about any of these was enough to get you thrown out of the park. Within my first month, the Kalakkad ranger came to see me. He wanted a letter from me, saying cattle-grazing was good for the park. It was my duty to give it to him, since the local people were suffering because of the newly imposed ban! On my next visit to Sengaltheri, I met with hostility from some people who stopped me on the road. The ranger had taken Rs 500 (a princely sum in those days) from them to give to me to have the ban lifted! Since nothing had happened, they assumed that I had just taken the money and done nothing. However, it all got sorted out with them at last. A few days later I met the then Conservator of Forests, S.M.A. Aslam, a gem of a person, by accident, and the ranger disappeared for good. After that, Mr Aslam kept an eye on me to make sure I wasn't bothered, although to him, the idea of pursuing research on monkeys was hilarious.

When the Mundanthurai Sanctuary was brought under the Wildlife Division of the forest department, the District Forest Officer (DFO) had a brainwave. He transferred every troublemaker in his division to the areas that would come under the Wildlife Division. It took twenty years or more for the damage to be repaired.

With the newly formed Wildlife Division, two new wildlife posts were created. One was for Mundanthurai, while the other was for the newly formed Kalakkad Sanctuary. This sanctuary was established based on a US researcher's personal letter to the then

Prime Minister, Indira Gandhi, explaining its importance for Lion-tailed macaque conservation.

At least the two new wildlife wardens appointed were interested in wildlife, and small steps were initiated. A crackdown on grazing and firewood collection started, and this took almost three decades to be fully implemented. Even today, there are cattle ostensibly belonging to tribals in the park (actually they belong to a local politician). However, as even today, how well the park was run depended entirely on the wildlife wardens. Some of them were very sincere, some obviously corrupt; many were honest but with absolutely no knowledge of wildlife and no readiness to learn either.

My relationship with the park authorities was by and large negative. Here was somebody who appeared to have contacts with their bosses, and reported every incident in the forest to them. The bosses, one of whom had four unmarried daughters and needed to make dowry money for them quickly, were a ready and willing audience for nasty stories about me. I was often asked to vacate my room at a moment's notice and move somewhere else when a VIP came, for they were afraid that I would share my stories with them. Once, a new DFO called me and asked me whether it was true that I stole chappals! By the time I had finished writing my PhD and returned, stories had spread about my undesirability, and I was denied permission to work. There was no chance of converting anything I'd done into a long-term project.

The next major administrative change occurred when both the parks became Kalakkad Mundanthurai Tiger Reserve (KMTR) and were brought under the aegis of Project Tiger. This exercise started off with a lie. The presence of at least twenty tigers was necessary for an area to be included under Project Tiger; our compilation of existing sightings suggested that there were no more than eight. The number rose every year, since the field director had to show an increase. When I got involved with the park again in 1994, the figure was twenty-nine. Promode Kant was the field director at the time; one of the finest forest officers I have had the privilege to meet. He and I discussed the matter at length. I expressed scepticism of the inflated figure and he agreed to review it, possibly to a more acceptable figure. But, perhaps mindful of repercussions for his colleagues and wanting to avoid making his boss too unhappy, he revised it only to twenty-two.

What were the researchers doing, allowing these estimates to go through? We were questioned and asked by journalists and others to prove it. Now, it is easy to show a difference between tiger and no tiger, but difficult to show the difference between fifteen and twenty-five of them, especially using the old pugmark method, which was the only government accepted method of proof. Ultimately, it took the extinction of tigers in Sariska to blow the lid off this scam.

In spite of all this, KMTR was probably the most researcher-friendly park in the country. At least twenty PhDs have been produced from there, notwithstanding tribulations, such as a researcher's entire studygroup of the Nilgiri langur getting poached and eaten by the ranger in his absence. However, the change came about with Promode Kant becoming the field director—he actively began encouraging researchers, even though they were frowned upon in the rest of Tamil Nadu.

Madhusudan Katti studied warblers at KMTR, and was constantly teased by Promode Kant about how his research had no conservation value. To this, Madhu had replied with a fabulously written, thought-provoking piece called 'Are Warblers Less Important than Tigers?'*

Promode was also a very supportive field director, particularly seen in the case where Mahesh Sankaran wanted to try out experimental burns over small bits of grassland. Although Promode was helpful, convincing the Chief Wildlife Warden would have been a problem. After a month's long wait for the permit, I myself

---

* Also included in this collection.

made a call to the Warden. He acknowledged that the issue had major conservation implications but also highlighted that he could get into trouble for clearing it. Was there any way I could convince Mr Sankaran to do more replicates, rather than just one, since another opportunity might not come again? That should not be a problem, I thought, and the research started.

A few more researchers wished to work on bonnet macaques. The Chief Wildlife Warden, at one stage, was reluctant to give the permits. So I called him again some time later only to be told that there was no conservation value in the study of bonnet macaques. I reminded him of my own study on the species and its conservation value. And the permits came through.

However, years later I could no longer recognize most of the study animals in my group. A number of large, strange males had joined in, apparently shattering one of my pet theories, that it was the females who migrated from group to group. Also, the tension levels in the group always seemed to be very high. It turned out that Mundanthurai had become a dumping ground for problematic macaques from the plains. Now, these males make life miserable for anyone who goes to the resthouse.

It has been a privilege being associated with the same area for almost forty years now. It's a pity I didn't keep detailed field notes during this time, since many of the changes I observed could only have been documented over long periods. The chital were abundant; they almost went extinct; now they have bounced back. Wild dogs, once abundant, are seldom seen. The ranges of the common langurs have shifted upriver. These are no more than impressions, since I do not have the notes to back them. The moral, to all young researchers: keep a field notebook and update it daily!

Are Warblers Less Important than Tigers?

MADHUSUDAN KATTI

Now, what kind of a stupid question is that! Everyone knows that tigers are more important. They are the large predators, apex species right at the top of the food chain, flagship species for conservation, etc… etc…

These are the arguments thrown at me when I tell people I am studying warblers in the Kalakkad Mundanthurai Tiger Reserve. For some reason, studying these tiny, nondescript, common birds is thought to be an entirely trivial, indeed arcane, academic pursuit of little practical or conservation value.

'What can studying little birds tell me about the habitat of large mammals, which are my primary concern?' asked the reserve manager. On the other hand, if we focus on the larger mammals—the apex species philosophy of Project Tiger—and do our best to improve their habitat, other species will naturally benefit. Given limited funds and manpower for conservation, research and action, is it not better to focus on the mega-fauna and let the mini- and micro-fauna take care of themselves? The only small creatures one should then worry about are those that may form part of the food chain leading up to the larger focal species.

Before you accuse me of a biased perspective (which is undoubtedly true, for I make my living watching little warblers!), let me state that in defending these little creatures, I am also arguing in favour of a broader ecological perspective in conservation—one that goes beyond the charismatic mega-fauna, and looks at species in terms of their ecological role in the system, rather than their appearance/charisma, or tourism potential.

So, what is the ecological role of my little leaf warblers?

Leaf warblers (Genus *Phylloscopus*) surely rank among the least glamorous vertebrates, so utterly lacking in charisma that even many die-hard birdwatchers dismiss them lightly, scarcely bothering to try and even identify them at the species level. Part of the problem is, of course, the fact that they are all small, dull-green coloured and highly active in the forest canopy, making identification in the field difficult. It is only rarely—either when one is obsessed about birds or when the fate of one's PhD thesis hangs on such identification— that one develops the eye for the subtle morphological, auditory and behavioural differences between species. These difficulties in identifying the species, however, need not bother our busy manager too much, since they (the leaf warblers) are all pretty similar ecologically as well; the role they play in the forest is largely independent of their taxonomic status, except insofar as structural aspects of their foraging micro-habitat within the forest canopy are concerned.

All eighteen species of leaf-warblers found in the Indian subcontinent are migratory. They breed in the temperate summers from north of the Himalayas to the Arctic Circle, and take over the peninsular forests (including the Himalayan foothills and much of north-east India) from September, through May. While each individual may weigh only 7–11 grams (the range includes all species), one may still emphasize the term 'take over', when describing their relationship to their forest habitats. They number in the billions and form probably the most abundant avian guild in the subcontinental forests during our tropical winter. My study at Mundanthurai (in the southern Western Ghats) records a density of six to eight leaf warblers (of two species) per hectare of forest. Usually any given patch of forest may have two to three species, depending on the type of forest; and I doubt there is any forest habitat in India that does not host at least one species some time of the year. Picking a random hectare from my 20-hectare study plot at Mundanthurai, I found six leaf warblers (belonging to two species) making it their home for about eight months, for these are territorial individuals that remain on-site for much of the winter. And what do they do during this period? Well, eat insects mostly! Humdrum as their lives may sound, they spend over 75 per cent of their waking hours foraging predominantly for insects, and other arthropods, in the foliage. Since they are not concerned about finding mates or raising young during this season, and want merely to survive in good shape for the next summer, their other activities—preening and maintaining territories through vocal and visual dialogue with neighbours—do not keep them very busy. A bunch of small, dull birds spending most of their day peering at leaves in search of insects—do I seem to be only weakening the defence? Not really...

Let us consider the fact that each leaf warbler, on averaging out all its activities throughout the day, eats three insects every waking minute. Since they forage by picking prey off a substrate—mostly leaves, sometimes also twigs and flowers—the prey largely consists of herbivorous insects. In the case of my 1 hectare on Mundanthurai, it is mostly caterpillars eating leaves. A single leaf warbler eats 180 insects every hour, or about 1980 per day (assuming an average eleven-hour working day from dawn to dusk). The six individuals on the plot thus rid the plants of almost 12,000 insect pests every day! Multiply that with the number of days (200–250) that they are in residence on that 1-hectare plot and you may begin to appreciate the service they render to all the plants. Now remove these warblers from the study plot, since they seem to take away so much research and conservation energy from the more favoured mammals, and picture the forest as it may appear in a few weeks' time! The scenario could become even more dramatic if, in the grip of large-mammal chauvinism, all the other insectivorous birds are removed from the plot as well. I estimate each hectare of Mundanthurai's forest has at least forty insectivorous birds, including other warblers and flycatchers (both resident and migrant), minivets, shrikes, drongos, babblers, among others. The average number of prey may come down to just over two per bird per minute that amounts to a total of about 5,000 insects per hour, or 55,000 per day in each hectare of forest! Remove those insectivores...and don't be surprised if in a few weeks the plants start to appear ragged with their foliage tattered, and your endangered langurs become unhappy because so many leaves are now covered with toxic anti-herbivore compounds produced in response to caterpillar nibblings; if the plants bear fewer flowers and fruits as they are forced to spend most of their energy in self-defence, in turn making the nectarivores and frugivores unhappy; and regeneration of the forest slows down as fewer seeds get produced and dispersed, and the ground starts to dry faster because the canopy is thinner and more sunlight filters in. I leave you to work out the rest of the ecological cascade effects! For now, I'd be happy if you simply pause to appreciate the job done by the nondescript little green leaf warblers and their insectivore colleagues that travel thousands of kilometres every year to accomplish it.

Before you start protesting that no one will ever contemplate removing all those birds and that I am just another doomsayer, consider the fact that 80 per cent of the warblers (especially the green leaf warbler, which is the most common one here) as well as the next most abundant migrant (Blyth's reed warbler), spending each winter at Mundanthurai, come from the hill forests around the Caspian Sea, from Turkey east through Kashmir, including bits of southern Russia and Afghanistan. Now imagine that these hills—breeding grounds for so many migrant insectivores—are deforested on a large scale, either directly by us or indirectly through climate change, thereby reducing the bird population by 90 per cent. Such cases are not very unrealistic, as those studying migrant forest birds in the Americas will tell you, although they worry more about deforestation in the wintering areas rather than in the breeding grounds. In fact, over the past two decades, Americans and Europeans are increasingly facing the prospect of another *Silent Spring*. Not, this time, due to the factors mentioned in Rachel Carson's clarion call in the 1960s—the over-use of chemicals in agriculture at the height of the green revolutions—but to a suite of other human activities that have hit the habitat of avian migrants in both their northern breeding grounds and southern wintering grounds. Many species of migrant songbirds, which enliven the northern spring after the dreary and silent winters, have been pushed to the brink of extinction over the past two decades—some like the Kirtland's warbler down to a few scores of breeding pairs, even as my ornithologist comrades in the West are racing against time to figure out the causes of these declines in order to reverse the process! The culprits are, of course, us humans—deforesting the tropical wintering grounds, fragmenting the temperate forests into suburban woodlots more accessible to human subsidized nest-predators such as domestic cats and other small carnivores (wild or feral) thriving on our garbage, and directly subsidizing the populations of non-migratory nest-parasites like the North American cowbird through back-yard bird-feeders, enabling them to survive the harsh winter, and fool over 200 gullible species of songbirds into raising their offspring. We seem to be particularly adept at causing damage to the ecological fabric of this planet, even when we mean good—feed them, poor little birdies, in the winter or the cute raccoons at night!

With respect to our continent, where we have no information on the population trends of forest birds—whether resident or migratory, in tropical south and south-east Asia or temperate Russia, Mongolia and Siberia—declines paralleling those in the other continents are very much on the cards, that is, if they have not occurred already! Given the contempt that these migrants have for human geopolitical boundaries, their populations are subject to forces beyond the control of any one national conservation agency, let alone the manager of a single tiger reserve. And, if their populations are found to be declining as drastically as many New World migrants' have over the past several decades, mammal chauvinists may be reduced to haplessly watching the habitats of their favourite creatures getting degraded.

Do you think even the tigers might get worried about such a scenario?

Is it worth studying these warblers then, trying to figure out what makes their populations thrive and how to save them, and ensure they continue to keep all those insects in check?

'Are warblers less important than tigers?'—isn't the question itself meaningless?

Lunch with the Snow Leopard

YASH VEER BHATNAGAR

I stand on top of the Phooma ridge at 5,200 metres and look around. With the 360-degree view from this sharp ridge, I begin to discover the layout of the land that I am to cover in the next five years, trying to understand the ecology of the Asiatic ibex. These are the early 1990s, before Google Earth was invented, when the Survey of India's photocopied topographic sheets were the only maps that were available. These maps are detailed, but for the uninitiated, they do not allow a good feel of the landscape. However, the positive side of not having a good map is that you can take on the role of an explorer and go from valley to ridge top, to another valley and develop the idea into a map of your own. Phooma is an ideal place for me to start as it is located towards the eastern exit of the Parahio valley and offers a complete upstream view of my study area, covering about 400 square kilometres. The Khaminger nala, coming from the edge of the Bara Shigri glacier to the north, meets the Debsa nala, which emerges from the Pir Panjal range above the Parbati valley in Kullu, to form the Parahio river. Parahio is joined by the Killung nala, from the south, and a few other streams on both banks that include the Phooma, Kocho and Gechang nalas and finally, the Kidul Chu river, before it joins the Pin river at the Sagnam village. I can now see most of these areas and form a mental picture of the land. Suddenly the topsheet also begins to make a lot of sense. I feel that I know the area now.

Phooma is a very small valley, right opposite to my base camp—a beautiful hamlet called Gechang in the heart of the Pin Valley National Park in Spiti, Himachal Pradesh. There are just two houses here, and people arrive in the valley in the month of May to cultivate barley and peas and also to herd some livestock, and then leave immediately after the biggish snowfall begins in November. One of these houses belongs to Dorje Zangpo, who is now working as our assistant. An extremely meticulous person, Zangpo is very creative and always ready to learn. He manages the camp very well and frequently adds value by making a stone bench, a flowerbed or diverting the streamlet to get running water at the camp. He also remembers the scientific names of all plants, much to my relief, as I keep forgetting the names every winter when they are all buried in several feet of snow. Chimmed Dorje is my other assistant. A simple and good-natured man, Chimmed shares Zangpo's interest in the area and in our work too. Both are well acquainted with the objective of my study and can locate ibex kilometres away, and understand how we characterize the habitat where they occur. As a bonus, both love cooking, especially rajma and cheese parantha, and many local dishes, including a variety of local cuisine such as *que* and *pak*.

I am in the Pin valley with a colleague, Nima Manjrekar, as a part of the Wildlife Institute of India's pioneering study on ibex ecology. If all goes well, we should be able to learn about the ibex's needs in terms of forage plants, topographic conditions, human pressure and so on. We even hope to capture some ibexes to study their ranging patterns; the home range required by them, their selection of these home ranges, differences between the sexes and so on. Obtaining permits for the collaring part takes time, so we must begin studying the ibex in the good old traditional way of finding them and observing them to record data. Although it gives us immense joy, it can often become quite tedious.

I monitor trails or transects that are typically 8–10 kilometres long and go along valleys and crests, with the primary goal being to maximize the view around. I need to try and quickly reach the end of the transect making all observations on the way, at times stopping at vantage points from where a large area is visible. At every sighting, I mark the location of the animals on the map, characterize the habitat and note their activity and any signs of human pressure in the vicinity. This data, collected over a season, tells us the likely set of ideal features for the ibex in different seasons, or even, about what the ibex might prefer. Ibexes are relatively common and safe in their range in India and one of the goals of understanding the ecology of the ibex is to gain an understanding of the ecology of the apex predator of the area—the elusive snow leopard. In the past, many romantic writings have been dedicated to this species, including Peter Mattiessen's *Snow Leopard*, and many epithets have been given to this animal, like that of a 'grey ghost' by the famous biologist, George Schaller. I am more of a 'dog person', and this elusive cat occupied only a peripheral space in my interests. The geology, plants, the ibex and the local people occupied most of my fascination.

As is expected of wild goats, the ibex also mostly forage close to the cliffs, primarily to escape predators like the snow leopard and the Tibetan wolf. Given my experience of shy animals in forested areas, I initially tried to stalk the ibex to get close to them. However, I soon understood that it was an impossible task; in spite of taking all precautions on the steep, crumbly slopes, some sound was inevitable and the ibex would get startled and scamper into the cliffs. It was a bit later that I realized that since the local people do not really disturb animals, the best way to approach an ibex is to walk slow, diagonally towards it in their full view. This way, they would just keep a safe distance of 15–20 metres. But when they get startled and run into the cliffs is a sight to behold—the ease and speed with which they jump and negotiate on what may be a smooth 80-degree cliff and easily manage to find a foothold. Any predator will find it very difficult to match their agility on these cliffs. My data indicated that there were some lush pastures far from cliffs, but these were never or rarely used by ibexes; instead, the scanty ones interspersed within cliffs were preferred. They seem to trade off abundant forage for greater security.

The onset of winter posed a huge challenge for my research, with temperatures dropping to -40 degrees Celsius coupled with strong winds, heavy snowfall and poor logistics that threatened to halt my work. I needed to overcome these challenges and recognized that there were ways of achieving this. For the cold, besides arranging for suitable clothing and heating in the camp, one just has to start enjoying it!

Zangpo and Chimmed were initially reluctant to stay back in Gechang for the winter but eventually realized that if an outsider was willing to risk a stay, they surely could. I remain forever indebted to them for the decision, as without this, my study wouldn't have been possible and I would have missed what clearly became my favorite time of the year. We worked out systems to look at each problem and overcome them. Our bunker, a small, loosely built stone structure with two rooms, was carefully mended; we looked for cracks in the wall and repaired them. We bought a few yak loads of fuelwood from the forest department, and Zangpo and Chimmed carefully prepared a long list of rations that we stocked up in November while the roads were still open. I realized that the scope of gathering information about the ibex was tremendous during this season; it was impossible to miss an ibex sighting as their tracks would show up clearly on the snow as would their dark bodies. It made the viewing in a huge area as this possible. We used racquet-shaped snowshoes to build our own paths on the 4–5 feet deep snow. The first person would usually face the greatest difficulty in 'opening' a route, while the other two compressed the track to create a path on the sheet of snow a few feet above the ground. In subsequent monitoring we could just follow this path quite fast. Any wavering from the path would land us waist-deep in snow.

Nima tried to find out what the ibexes ate. The usual process was to look at feeding sites and see which plants were eaten as against what was available there. Here, however, one had to reach the spot immediately after the animals left the site. It was difficult to identify if the feeding signs were that of the ibex or some livestock that may have grazed upon the same site. The other method was to collect ibex dung and, through a lab-based process of drying and grinding it, make slides and classify the fragments to identify plant species under a microscope. With so many different possibilities for species and plant parts, this was no easy task. The winter presented us with an interesting opportunity. I noticed that almost all the foraging happened by way of digging small craters through snow. The animals would be seen sinking their muzzles a few inches into the snow in a way to feel or sniff out a plant, and on finding some forage they would stand there and dig using their forelegs. As the plant appeared, they would begin feeding on it, thereby spending considerable time at each crater. These craters then provided accurate information on what exactly was foraged on. But there were challenges here too. The ibex here mostly used higher slopes throughout winter and did not descend as is expected of many similar species. One obvious reason was that the lower elevations were covered in deep snow, mostly thicker and more compact than what occurred on the steeper slopes. Further, the upper elevations had numerous ridges and crests where some snow had blown off, leaving behind a thinner layer of snow. Ibexes also spend considerable time foraging on the avalanche chutes, areas from where avalanches trigger in the upper slopes, which results in a thinner layer of snow. I decided to monitor these craters to see if we could document what was eaten. Soon I began finding interesting information on ibex foraging during the winter season. I checked most craters at a feeding station and also dug up numerous sites to see what species were available there. I listed the plants that clearly seemed to be preferred and all of these—grasses, sedges and other herbs—had only one common feature: they were all erect in habit. Other species of plants were also present but were smothered on to the ground by the thick layer of snow and were thus not really available to the animals, even though they had much greater cover.

What I realized during the process was that ibex forage on almost anything that they can get their muzzles on. Other studies also confirm that during winter, ruminants mainly look for some forage to fill their stomach and do not select it based on the nutritional value of the plant, a pattern reserved mainly for the abundance of summer.

Besides offering a phenomenal view of the entire region and satiating our curiosity for the ways of the ibex, the Phooma ridge was covered with fresh signs of the presence of a snow leopard; its scats, scrapes and other evidences strewn all over. The place gave a thrilling sense of the predator being very close. It seemed to like the place for the same reason as mine—the excellent views and the ibex population in the vicinity.

Another feature that captured my attention was that here, one could walk on an ancient seabed. A section of the ridge top is a huge slanting slab, over half a kilometre in length, containing the fossils of ammonites and nautiloids. Geologists call Spiti valley an open library. The initiated can easily read nature, an open book in itself, and spot the upheavals, the deep sea bed, a shallow section of the Tethys sea, the point where a steep stream must have joined the sea, and so on. The area bears witness to the history of the period from the Cambrian (c. 540 million years ago), when simple marine multi-cellular organisms appeared, the Silurian—when arthropods such as trilobites became common, to the Cretaceous—when the ammonites flourished in the seas while dinosaurs dominated the land, spanning a period of over 500 million years. The period when the Indian Plate separated from Gondwana land around 130 million years ago (in the early Cretaceous) and began its 6000 kilometre journey to its present alignment, thrusting under the Eurasian plate, uplifting the Tibetan Plateau and later resulting in the formation of the Greater Himalayan chain (c. 48 million years ago, in the Paleocene) are all included in this library. A bit of reading and interaction with the visiting geologists opened up these mysteries to me, but only slightly. One can only sit and wonder how these beautiful ridges and valleys came into formation led by the intense and mysterious forces of nature!

It was a cold winter morning in February. The previous night had seen temperatures touching -35 degrees Celsius, but the sun was out now. It was ten in the morning and the temperature in the mild sunshine was still at -4 degrees. All of us set out behind Gechang to the area above what we had named the 'Concave Rock', a mass of cliffs on the right bank of the stream, the largest face of which was concave. Above this were some lush meadows, mainly, ricegrass (Oryzopsis) and feathergrass (Stipa) that cover these slopes for over 200 metres till the ridgeline, which was a jumbled mass of cliffs. I had been studying the behavioural patterns of ibexes in this group from dawn to dusk for the past four days and decided to take a look at what they had been eating by looking inside their feeding craters.

From the camp we could see the slopes above the Concave Rock but we did not notice the ibex there. I began to wonder what might have happened. We observed the group till about five last evening when it had become dark and they had already settled down for their night's rest below the cliffs along the ridgeline. In winter, ibexes normally leave their resting sites for foraging only after ten or eleven in the morning when they forage for three to four hours before settling down for the night. I had also noticed that the ibex would normally stay at one site for five to seven days, before moving on to another site in a single file, and then on, further through the winter. This is probably to optimize on the effort of reaching a slope and maximizing on consuming all forage that is available there. 'But where have they gone so early today?' That was the question in my mind as we set out for the stiff climb along the edge of the Concave Rock. I asked Chimmed to climb higher to a small rock outcrop to see if he could locate the ibex group, while Zangpo and I began our sampling in the vast foraging area. Some time later, we saw Chimmed excitedly running down the slope with something heavy on his back. As he reached closer, I noticed a yearling female ibex, only partially eaten by a predator, with fresh wounds on her body. The Spitians are pious Buddhists and do not indulge in killing animals for meat, but they do love to eat meat that they didn't have to kill! Stealing the kills of predators or scavenging avalanche kills thus, are a very common part of their quest for meat. I could see the delight on Chimmed and Zangpo's faces—they had stocked up with some frozen yak meat, but had to do with the rajma, black dal, soya nuggets and potatoes that I had stocked up for the winter. 'Nothing like fresh meat,' they explained. I felt miserable to deny them, but it couldn't be allowed. I checked the throat and it was clear that the animal had been killed by the throat bite of a snow leopard. I explained why it was not right for us to steal this kill from the snow leopard—given the harsh winter, a lot of effort must have gone in to stalk and kill the healthy ibex. The leopard had just disemboweled the ibex and had hardly eaten a few pounds of flesh from the left flank. If we took its kill, no one knows when the creature would get another chance. They agreed to put the carcass of the ibex back where it was found. While this was being done, I realized that the snow leopard surely must be around observing us, maybe even now as this thought passed my mind! It increased my excitement, as I realized that this might give us a chance to see the leopard at its kill. The kill was kept at exactly the same place under the small overhang where I had asked Chimmed to go and look around. This point was visible from Gechang. We scanned the upper slopes and could see numerous tracks running down the slope from the cliffs above towards the concave rock. We began inspecting and in time, were able to reconstruct the happenings of the previous night. We located snow leopard pugmarks and a resting site, or must have been a patient crouching site, just about 10 metres above where we had seen the ibex group settle down last night. It must have made a dash for the ibex group resting close below the largest mass of cliffs, in a manner that cut their retreat into the cliffs above. The animals ran amok straight downslope, the leopard in hot pursuit. About 30 metres below, the leopard cut to its right and isolated the yearling, which tried to run sideways to the left. We found signs of struggle within a few metres and a small patch of frozen blood. The drag mark from here to the outcrop was clear. We had managed to reconstruct the events of the previous night just like Corbett and were mighty thrilled at this. We completed our crater study and as we traced our way back to Gechang, I began thinking about what this meant for my study. I realized the fact that proximity to cliffs doesn't provide enough safety to the ibex. Snow leopards can attack from the top, and if they cut the only retreat into the cliffs, the ibex are vulnerable and have to find escape in another distant cliff. The only possibility is that if the ibex chooses areas that have cliffs in more than one direction, then a solitary predator can only cut off one retreat, leaving more possibilities for escape. I immediately decided to add another variable to the data I collected at each ibex sighting—that of the number of directions in which cliffs were available within 100 metres of the group, with a maximum possible direction being eight (top, bottom, right, left, top-right, top-left and so on). Interestingly, out of over 800 sightings about 90 per cent were within 100 metres from the cliffs, of which most were at sites where there were cliffs in three to four directions. The cliffs themselves were avoided as they hardly have any forage. Similarly, areas in its proximity that had just one or two escape routes were also used relatively lesser. A small, but interesting fact about the ibex.

We were awake early next morning and Zangpo had set up the spotting scope even before dawn. My wife, Krishna, who is from the warm state of Andhra Pradesh and was with me during most of the study, was all geared up for her first sighting of the snow leopard. As the first rays of the sun came over the mountains, Zangpo strained his eyes through the scope, frequently zooming in and out. He was concentrating on the outcrop, as that was where we expected the leopard to be—just above the kill. After an hour passed by, we finally located the magnificent animal. It was there, sure enough, but had its head down, and was completely camouflaged against the rock. Just as it raised its head, it became vaguely visible in the constantly fogging scope. We were thrilled. The leopard was at its kill! We declared it a 'holiday' and decided to climb the slope behind Gechang, from where we could have a direct view of the leopard. All four of us set out with warm clothing, shovels and carry mats to make ourselves comfortable, as comfortable as one could get in the freezing temperatures with a constant breeze blowing upslope. We dug up a trench in the snow and must have been about half a kilometre opposite the leopard. It stared at us quizzingly but soon decided to ignore us and went into deep slumber. I constantly maintained an activity pattern of the animal every ten minutes, which read somewhat like 'sleeping, sleeping, sleeping, moving right forelimb, looking at us, sleeping on its left side, sleeping, sleeping, sleeping, sleeping, yawning, sleeping, sleeping...' While we were at it, Zangpo rushed back to the camp and got a flask of hot tea and our primus stove. There, in the trench, he prepared delicious Maggie noodles with extra spices. It was an exhilarating experience—having tea and Maggie in the middle of a snow-covered slope, while occasionally looking into the eye of a snow leopard. We observed the leopard through the day. While looking at the leopard my mind drifted to what can easily be the most exciting moment of my two-decade career in wildlife. It was on this slope besides the Concave rock, during the first spring of my study. I looked at the small 'cave' with a triangular opening a little to the left of the Concave Rock.

One June morning, Chimmed and I started early to do some vegetation sampling on the same slopes above the Concave Rock. We located a fresh sheep kill near the stream-bed and a hot pursuit over crumbling slopes and steep shale screes had brought us to the edge of the Concave Rock. Chimmed, who was much faster, had gone up tracking the scanty spoor of the leopard and was now standing just above the cave. Totally breathless, I almost gave up on any chance of seeing the leopard and came on to a promontory some distance below where Chimmed was standing. As I stood there generally dejected with the effort, there was a sudden rush from the top and this elegant feline almost ran into me! Its startled round eyes looked at me and its long tail drawing an arch over its body, hit the back of its head. Whenever I remember this my thoughts decelerate into slow motion! I could even feel the whiff of its approach and the pebbles from its screeching halt hitting my arms. But like a ghost, in a couple jumps it went out of sight. We later realized that the leopard resting in the cave below was inadvertently disturbed by Chimmed and had run down, only to almost barge into me. What an encounter it was!

That was an amazing experience, similar to this one, sharing close proximity with the snow leopard, tolerating each other's presence. I felt good that we had left the kill behind for the leopard to enjoy. Zangpo and Chimmed also shared the same satisfaction. Snow leopards do get into conflict with herders over killing their livestock, and at times herders may persecute leopards. But all of us felt good that this leopard had its fill and maybe will not feel the need to hunt until next week.

I had begun to like snow leopards. They are mythical but approachable—becoming vulnerable, and in need of our help!

The Flight of the Amur Falcon

ANANDA BANERJEE

October 2013, Pangti (Nagaland): I am standing at the scene of a massacre like no other. Last year, like every year since 2006, a tenth of all Amur falcons were killed here. That's an estimated 10,000 to 14,000 a day for the ten days the birds spend in Nagaland, en route their winter migration from Russia to the southern part of Africa.

All around me, on trees, on the power lines across the village, are the falcons. This is the annual migration of the Amur falcons (*Falco amurensis*) over the Doyang reservoir in the Wokha district of Nagaland. I may well be witnessing one of nature's greatest spectacles. The number of birds is staggering and estimated at well over a million, although no one wants to put a number to it.

'This is probably the single largest congregation of Amur falcons recorded anywhere in the world,' said Ramki Sreenivasan, co-founder of Conservation India, a website dedicated to wildlife and nature conservation.

The birds are not endangered, but the species is protected under the Indian Wildlife Protection Act 1972, and the Convention on Migratory Species, to which India is a signatory (which means, it is mandatory for the state government to protect the birds), but conservationists worry that a few more years of the literal decimation of the species could make it critically so (the taxonomy of conservation recognizes species as vulnerable, endangered, and critically endangered, in increasing order of the threat they face and decreasing order of the number still alive).

In October 2012, to ascertain information on large-scale hunting in this remote region, Sreenivasan and Shashank Dalvi, research associates at the Centre for Wildlife Studies, and Bano Haralu and Rokohebi Kuotsu of the Nagaland Wildlife and Biodiversity Conservation Trust (NWBCT) visited Doyang to witness first-hand the massacre of Amur falcons on the banks of the Doyang reservoir.

Amurs are killed for food and for sale as food. Hunters set up nets on the roosting sites of the falcons on the banks of the reservoir. The birds are trapped either as they come in to roost in the evenings or leave the roost at dawn. The catch is removed every morning and transferred to mosquito nets or cane baskets so that the birds are alive (live birds fetch more).

The field trip by Sreenivasan and his associates—the first to officially record the massacre—alarmed conservationists.

In an article, 'How to make 2.5 billion termites disappear? A case for protecting the Amur Falcon', published in the 29 November 2012 online edition of *Ornithological Observations*, scientists Henk Bouwman, Craig Symes and Hannalene du Plessis establish that the Amur falcon's 'predatory nature may have consequences in its breeding and non-breeding areas. Large reductions in Amur Falcon numbers are therefore likely to have far reaching impacts on agriculture and the environment.'

For instance, the falcons reduce the number of African bollworm, a pest of sorghum in South Africa, and keep a check on the termite population. Further, 'any significant reduction in falcon numbers may have severe consequences on a sub-continental scale, potentially affecting millions of commercial and emerging farmers,' the authors warn.

A Unique Journey

The Amur falcon is a pigeon-sized, grey insectivorous raptor, locally known as Elinum (which refers to the wingbeats of a bird) in Nagaland. According to James Ferguson-Lees and David A. Christie (who wrote the book *Raptors of the World*), the population of the species is estimated at over a million.

According to the paper written by Andrew Dixon, Nyambayar Batbayar and Gankhuyag Purev-Ochir, 'Autumn Migration of an Amur Falcon *Falco amurensis* from Mongolia to the Indian Ocean tracked by satellite', that cites references from the published work of Ferguson-Lees and Christie, and other ornithologists, the species can be found from Transbaikalia, Russia and central Mongolia, east to Ussuriland (south-eastern Russian Far East) and south to the Qinling mountain range in central China.

'The species undertakes one of the most notable migrations of any bird of prey, departing their breeding grounds in late August and September, moving south through China, skirting the eastern edge of the Himalaya to reach north-east India and Bangladesh, where they settle temporarily to fatten before embarking through the Indian subcontinent and across the Indian Ocean to southern Africa. The unique non-stop journey of 3,000 kilometres across the Indian Ocean typically takes place in late November and December, aided by the prevailing easterly winds,' adds the paper.

The journey takes about four to five days. Bernd Meyburg, one of the leading experts on satellite tracking of raptors, has established that they fly 2,500–3,100 kilometres over the sea non-stop in two or three days.

In Nagaland, though, the bird is largely known as a source of food—and money.

Tajolo Lotha, fifty-two, a resident of Pangti village, claims that people earned Rs 25,000–35,000 last year from hunting falcons. His neighbour Zimomo Lotha, thirty-five, puts the sum even higher, between Rs 30,000–40,000. There are around fifty to sixty hunters in the village, Lotha added, and they sell at least 1,000 birds a day between them. Both Lothas are themselves hunters.

The hunting of Amur falcons provided a windfall gain to the otherwise marginalized Lothas of Pangti, Sungro and Ashaa.

This year, thanks to the effort of the Nagaland government, NWBCT and a few other non-governmental organizations (NGOs), and another independent initiative of the Wildlife Trust of India (WTI), the massacre has been stopped, although several issues remain unresolved.

Money is one: Seeking a safe passage

Earlier this year, the NWBCT, supported by the Nagaland government, Wildlife Conservation Society, Birdlife International, Bombay Natural History Society, Wildlife Conservation Trust and Raptor Research and Conservation Foundation, and Conservation India launched a wildlife education training programme, 'Friends of the Amur Falcon—Under the Canopy'.

'The state government is committed to end the unfortunate killings of the migratory Amur falcons and fully support the efforts of NWBCT and other NGOs to educate the people about these migratory birds and to give them a safe passage through Nagaland,' according to a statement from chief minister Neiphiu Rio.

'The Amur falcons are beautiful migratory birds, which visit Nagaland every year in thousands, in their long migratory journey from Siberia en route to South Africa covering 22,000 kilometres in a year. It is our duty to protect these wonderful birds while they are passing through Nagaland and treat them as our honoured and esteemed guests, in the true Naga tradition of hospitality,' said Rio.

Rio also threatened to shut off grants to villages that are involved in hunting the falcons.

'Various grants and assistance to villages that indulge in rampant killing and massacre of Amur falcons will be reviewed by the government and if required, the sanctions to such villages will be curtailed,' he said.

The government has also backed information campaigns with messages such as 'Protect Amur Falcons to save our global image', 'We carry the message of Globalization—let us not harm our visiting guests', with ground patrols and checks on local markets.

The church, which has a big say in Naga social life, is conducting special services on Sundays to spread the conservation message.

This particular message, 'These are the birds you are to regard as unclean and not eat because they are unclean: the kite, the falcon, of any kind, every raven of any kind, the ostrich, the nighthawk, the sea gull, the hawk of any kind, the little owl, the cormorant, the short-eared owl, the barn owl, the tawny owl, the carrion vulture, the stork, the heron of any kind, the hoopoe, and the bat', from the Book of Leviticus 11:13–19 has been put out by the church to change people's sensibilities.

And, in an effort to address the monetary aspect, in 2013, New Delhi-based WTI and its local partner, NGO Natural Nagas, entered into a Memorandum of Understanding (MoU) with the heads of the councils of three villages—Pangti, Sungro and Ashaa.

WTI did not share the Memorandum of Understanding (MoU), citing it as an 'internal document', but sent excerpts which read, 'The village council heads from these three villages have passed a resolution against hunting and trade of Amur falcons in Wokha, with a Rs 5,000 fine imposed on those caught doing so. An Amur Falcon Protection Squad has been set up, comprising groups of youth, many of whom are former hunters. This was an effort to involve local youth in conservation as well as to provide alternative livelihood as it had emerged that many of them were unemployed which had compelled them into hunting. Community support was provided in the form of a poultry farm to 30 families in Wokha who were part of the hunter groups and land owners. This was done not only to provide them an alternative source of income but also a legal source of protein (meat)'.

Brewing discontent

Villagers allege that they were not taken into confidence and only the chairman and his coterie has benefited from the MoU. Contrary to claims made by the chairman, people said that no meeting was called by the village council to discuss the MoU. When asked about the content of the MoU, the chairman of Pangti village, Ronchamo Shitri, said he doesn't have a copy and he hasn't even seen a final version of the document.

Now questions are being raised by villagers on the criteria used to select beneficiaries.

WTI has a separate MoU with the state's forest department, 'which includes assisting them in conservation initiatives in the state—Amur falcon conservation is one of them'.

Unlike elsewhere in the country, the forests here belong to the community, and this intrusion by the forest department and the NGO without involving the community has touched a raw nerve, hurting the Naga pride.

'Our work began with numerous interactions and meetings with the residents of Pangti, Ashaa and Sungro to make them aware of the need of such an initiative to save Amur falcons, which eventually culminated in the MoU that was signed with the village council heads,' said Dilip Deori, assistant manager, WTI, who helps with the coordination of the Rapid Action Project.

'The work is being done on the basis of the need for conservation of the falcons which is the priority in our agreement. Subsequent work—the kind of aid and beneficiaries—have been jointly decided and implemented with the village councils, who represent the people of these villages and know them and their need best, in consultation with the forest department authorities,' he said.

Between the two initiatives, the Amur falcons are flying free. But the situation in the three Lotha villages, Pangti, Sungro and Ashaa, the epicentre of last year's massacre, remains tense.

There is an undercurrent of discontent among a majority of people who made a living out of hunting falcons.

There's talk of compensation from the government as the birds are roosting on their land.

Santsuo Shitri, chairman of Ashaa village, claims that his village is the main roosting place for the falcons. Though the village donated land to the North-Eastern Electric Power Corp. Ltd. for the Doyang hydro-electric project, it has no power supply, he said. It will be difficult to control hunting without benefits for individuals and villages, he added. There are simply no jobs for the village youth, said Shirti.

Every household in the state has a gun because of the low licence fee; for sophisticated weapons it is only Rs 10 and renewal Rs 5, for breech-loading guns it is Rs 6 and renewal Rs 3, for muzzle-loading rifle and air guns it is Rs 4 and renewal Rs 2.

Zanthungo Shitio, president of the fishermen's union at Doyang, has a long list of demands which includes boats, fishing nets, life jackets and first aid kits.

The forest department is in the process of formulating a plan to improve the livelihoods of affected communities that focuses on eco-tourism, self-help groups, and the means of ensuring a sustainable livelihood.

The immediate challenge, according to NBWCT and Conservation India, is to remain engaged with the local population and see off the last of the migrants this year. The two have set up conservation education centres for this purpose (there are five centres, seventy students and twenty instructors).

By next year, if all goes well, the livelihood plan of the state government would have kicked in.

And the Amurs can avoid the fate of the central population, now declared extinct, of the Siberian crane that hasn't been seen in India for almost a decade, largely on account of hunting in Afghanistan and Pakistan, along the migratory route to India.

SECTION TWO:

FROM THE ARCHIVES

The Lonely Tiger

HUGH ALLEN

'Times have changed.'

Along one shelf in our library are the books on shikar that helped to bring me to Mandikhera. They go back to 1858, exactly a hundred years, and in most of them that phrase crops up repeatedly. Nearly all the writers use it, and with few exceptions, they use it before going on to lament the growing scarcity of game.

A lot certainly has changed in the last hundred years and the game has indeed grown steadily scarcer. Just how much scarcer is shown strikingly between the first book on the shelf and the last. In the first, published during the Mutiny, the author was a Lieutenant William Rice, who tells of shooting ninety-eight tigers, four leopards and twenty-five bears during one hot weather furlough. In the last book, on a shoot of about the same length of time, the writer admits he was lucky and well content with two tigers and one leopard.

Essay taken from: Allen, Hugh. *The Lonely Tiger* (New Delhi: Rupa Publications India Pvt. Ltd., 1960), pp. 126–143.

The books written in the decade or so following the Mutiny show the gradual changes as they came. One of the main changes was brought about by the swift and terrible punishment meted out for the revolt. When that was over and the stick finally hung behind the door, it was at last safe for sportsmen to wander even in the remotest jungles. That, perhaps, was the golden age of Indian shikar: the animals were in their hundreds, and although the only weapon was still the muzzle-loader, the slaughter was incredible. Then, as the ramrod and powder-horn gave way to the breech-loader and the magazine rifle, some of the old ideas of sport started to change, too. Game was still plentiful, but some sportsmen now began to realize that it might not last forever, if weapons became even handier and more powerful.

Not much later, every serious writer was a little worried. The animals really *were* being thinned down. There was, of course, still plenty of sport, but now come the first pleas to make it last and the first criticisms of the over-keen sportsmen that never knew when they'd had enough. Another menace these writers noted was the growing number of 'native gunners over waterholes', and they suggested a drastic curtailment of the muzzle-loaders allowed for crop protection.

Towards the closing years of British rule in India, there was real concern for the game. A lot of animals now were scarce and some kinds of them already well along the road to extinction. Even so, few of these later writers considered the position hopeless and most agreed about what should be done to improve it. A tightening of forest rules and stricter enforcement, a low limit to any individual's bag, more and larger game sanctuaries and—above all else—much more plain common sense.

Sound enough. In some other countries where the animals had been hunted as hard as they had been in India, prompt and energetic action had not only saved most of the game but seen it increase. The same thing would work here.

Then it was 1947, and with Independence times really *did* change. Old-time sportsmen, had they seen it, would have been speechless with amazement, for almost overnight an entirely new kind of hunter had started to roam the jungles. There had, of course, been black sheep before, but most hunters had obeyed the rules and shot in conventional ways. Not so the new men. Forest rules for them just did not exist and they shot neither on foot nor from a machan. Instead, they rode in a jeep, and as it sneaked along forest roads at night they picked off everything that showed up in the headlights from the comfort and security of the front seat.

At much the same time, the old 'water-hole gunner' really came into his own. The satanic government that had imposed those harsh measures to keep muzzle-loaders and 12-bores out of irresponsible hands, was gone. Now, almost anyone that cared to apply for a licence, was sure to get one. In no time at all, freshly killed venison was on display in the bazaars.

Indian sportsmen were aghast, and their letters of protest were soon flooding into newspaper offices. But they did little good; these sportsmen were a tiny minority and nothing they said or tried to do made the slightest difference: they were cranks from the bad old days.

This change came fast and its effects were noticeable almost at once. Indeed, looking back now it seems as though the animals disappeared overnight. All of them, of course, had not been shot. It was just that they were not seen about so often, and when they were seen, there was something about the way they fled that showed them sensible of the constant threat now abroad both by day and night.

It was not like this ten years ago. Then, herds of chital and nilgai were a common sight on any dawn round of the estate. Sambur would be about too, if you were early enough and in the right place, and there was hardly a morning that showed no glimpse of barking deer and four-horned antelope and the dainty chinkara sporting about the more open ravines.

Then the shots started to echo through the nights. Most of them were the long-drawn-out Boo-o-oom! of muzzle-loaders using the always-slightly-damp bazaar black powder. For the first few nights I believed it was just a sudden increase in the occasional poaching that has always worried us. But when the shots continued night after night, it was obvious that something unusual was going on.

A few inquiries soon showed what was happening. A lot of the small cultivators around us had acquired guns 'to protect their fields'. But they were not sitting over their crops. After dark most of them were roaming the forests in bullock-carts and shooting at any animal they met by the light of a torch. Along the main road that runs two miles from the estate, matters were even worse. At night this road is used by a lot of animals, which come out of the jungle on each side of it. Now, after them, went trucks and private cars creeping along in low gear with headlights blazing and a spot sweeping the sides—and perhaps as many as four gunners ready for the first pair of eyes to flash back at the lights.

These mechanized rogues had better weapons, shotguns with a sprinkling of old rifles. With these, the kills came easily. So did the money for skins, meat and horns. This was too much for the passengers in the local buses: such easy money could not be ignored and so these, too, began taking their weapons in case anything showed up along the way. An animal often did, and then an obliging driver—for a hunk of meat—would stop the bus and allow the shot to be taken through the window.

Most of the sportsmen who saw what was going on sent in reports. At first, though, they were not really worried for something like this was bound to happen when the old ban on firearms was suddenly lifted. Such flagrant poaching would, of course, not be allowed to go on; just let a few offenders be fined and have their arms confiscated and the abuses would stop. The authorities, when reports reached them, were bound to act quickly.

That the authorities did nothing was perhaps the biggest shock of all. The slaughter went on and there was not the slightest evidence that anything was being done to stop it. Nobody seemed to care, and as things got worse *The Times of India* came out with this:

'The Uttar Pradesh conference on the preservation of wild life has very appropriately drawn the country's attention to the depredations of poachers and trigger-happy shikaris. Herds of chital, chinkara and spotted deer have become rare and the reason for this, according to U.P.'s chief game warden, is the use of buckshot by shikaris who fire into a herd. For every animal that is killed on the spot, several others are injured by buckshot, and these beasts suffer a slow death from festering wounds. In parts of Uttar Pradesh poaching has apparently become organized business: in some towns of Lakhimpur Kheri district people seldom buy mutton; they prefer venison which is cheaper and readily available in the bazaar thanks to the very private enterprise of the poachers. Professional bird catchers are playing havoc with winged fauna and the conference was told that partridge and quail are on the verge of extinction. The Uttar Pradesh Government can be expected to accept the conference's recommendation that a two-year ban be imposed on the use of buck-shot and that the U.P. Birds and Wild Animals Protection Act be amended to put an end to the malpractices of the professional bird catchers. But this will not be enough.

Strengthening the law is no substitute for enforcing what is already on the statute book, and the conference revealed that the enforcement aspect has been neglected to an incredible extent. What is one to make of the official admission that a large number of poachers are Government servants? It is fair to assume that what is true of Uttar Pradesh is more or less true of other States. Government officials attending the Nainital conference were unable to suggest steps to put an end to this deplorable state of affairs. Divisional Commissioners and other senior revenue and police officials have promised to dissuade their subordinates from poaching, but persuasion is a curious method of enforcing the law.'

Right from the start, the poachers on our own land became an unmitigated nuisance. Very early on they got Leggy, a four-horned antelope, who screamed home one morning with a back leg hanging from a sinew after a meeting with a sneaking bullock-cart in the big nullah. Not long after, they got Sammy, a barking deer...

I saw some of the tragedy that was now getting into its stride from my wooden armchair above the pool in the nullah. This chair is built permanently into the fork of a giant tree and has been there nearly ten years. It is thirty feet above the pool and commands wide sweeps of the jungle beyond both banks. I use it a lot throughout the year and often spend whole nights in it watching the animals coming down to drink. The best time is towards the end of the hot weather. By then, the other pools in the nullah have dried up and this one holds the only water for a long way around.

The first hot weather after the change brought some of the tragedy now going on after dark into sharp focus. That year the mowha flowers were late. When at last they started to fall from hundreds of trees in a long strip of jungle near the pool, that was the only water for a considerable distance. At once, that strip became a death trap. The sweet fleshy petals of these flowers draw herbivorous animals like a magnet, and when the sickly sweet scent brought them to the strip, the bullock-carts were waiting in the darkness under the trees and on the road through it were the crawling trucks and jeeps.

The deer and antelopes were the hardest hit and brought to the pool the saddest stories of all. I would see fawns, which had been with their mothers a short time before suddenly appear alone, their eyes big and frightened in the moonlight; or a frantic hind, mad with anxiety, would come dashing down to the water searching desperately for a baby which would never nestle into her side again.

Nothing was being spared, and for every animal killed outright, several more got away wounded. Some of these staggered to the pool at their last gasp for a last drink. Others, not so badly hit, would come trembling with terror to quench a burning thirst. After doing that they would limp painfully away—perhaps to weeks of agony unless they were found and destroyed in the morning. For no shot is ever fired from the chair; the pool is a sanctuary and I like to believe that the animals know it.

It was late one night when I first saw the cub. He seemed to have come to the pool alone although he was obviously a very young tiger. By now, however, that was nothing unusual and he was very likely searching for a mother he would never find. Under the hard light of a full moon, I watched him flitting about by the water's edge. He seemed quite happy, and if his solitary state concerned him he was not showing it. He was not thirsty either for he made no attempt to drink but just played with the dead leaves rustling on the sand in the light breeze.

I was just wondering how to catch him in the morning when his mother materialized from the shadows under the left bank of the nullah. As she came, another cub was playing with her tail. She went straight to the pool and drank, then the three glided away as silently as they had come.

The next evening, I was up in the chair early. The night before, those cubs had looked young enough for that outing to have been one of their first. If that was true, it suggested a hideout close to the pool and the tigress would certainly come again. But as the moon was bright and she would come up warily, I had taken Bimbo with me and tied him in the branches above my head.

Bimbo is a langur monkey who hates all the big cats. For this reason, he often earns his keep because the merest glimpse of a tiger or leopard sets him screaming his lungs out and dancing about the tree like a drunken dervish. That kind of performance is often useful to put a suspicious animal at ease if it has either seen or heard anything unusual from where you are sitting. But once Bimbo starts his act there can be no doubt—he was only a monkey after all.

The tigress came soon after nine o'clock and Bimbo was off the moment she appeared. But this time it didn't work for when the tigress looked up she must have spotted me at once. She did not come to the pool again for more than two months; rather than expose her cubs to a possible risk she drank at the river some way to the south. It was on a night much later when I did not expect them that the three glided down to the pool again. That was the last time I saw the tigress alive. When I saw her next, she was stretched on the concrete floor of a garage twenty miles away. A truck driver had shot her the previous night.

When I found the tigress in the garage I was on my way to Jubbulpore for three days. Had it been possible to skip my appointment I should have gone straight back to look for the cubs. As it was, I could only wonder what had become of them all the time I was away. If they had been close to their mother when she was killed either of two fates could have overtaken them: they might have been shot or captured. The last possibility was the more likely. Tiger cubs are a rich prize and they are not difficult to round up because all young animals suddenly losing mothers will hang about the spot where she disappeared from for several days.

Those cubs had been so much on my mind that I went down to the pool shortly after I got home and began to search along the water's edge. I was not really expecting to find any sign of them, but almost at once I found their small pug marks and near them, half buried in the sand, a chewed peacock's feather with traces of blood. An hour later, I had found more feathers and the remains of a full-grown peacock.

The cubs were safe after all and obviously needed no help from me. The wily peacock is difficult to surprise, and to have got one, the cubs must already be using 'big tiger' tactics and haunting the game-paths leading to the water. They could safely be left on their own, but to keep an eye on them I meant to find their hideout.

It was a good place. The tigress had chosen well and was rearing them in a deep cave with a narrow slit of an entrance well screened with thorns on the side of a hill. It was, as I had suspected, not far from the pool; yet I might never have found it but for the lucky accident of seeing, from some high ground a little way off, one of the cubs coming out.

Once I knew where they lived, I got to know them well with glasses from that high ground. They grew fast, and it was not long before they were hunting bigger game; nor was it long before they were roaming farther afield. Then they started staying away from the cave for days at a time. I was sorry about that; they had been a source of endless delight and this meant that they would not be staying much longer for they were now big enough to split up.

At last, I thought they had gone. More than a week went by and there had been no sign of them near the cave. But most evenings I climbed to the high ground and searched with the glasses. Then one evening they were back and I knew that they had killed something near the entrance to the cave. The clue was vultures waiting patiently on a silk-cotton tree halfway up the hill.

I enjoy stalking, so I set off to get near enough to watch them on whatever they had killed. After some time, I picked up the young tigress lying on some grass in a patch of shade. But of the tiger and the kill there was no sign, although I spent another fifteen minutes looking round for them.

I was just starting to turn back when I felt that something was wrong. For a few seconds I thought that sixth sense was a warning of danger; the tiger now was big enough to be rough if he caught me near his kill. Before moving, I glanced all round me and then climbed higher up the hill. There was still no sign of him, but from my new position I saw on the ground below me some vultures I had not noticed before. A moment later I realized the truth. There was no kill and the vultures were hopping slowly towards the tigress because she was dead.

Her body was still warm. She could not have died much more than an hour before. Her white stomach, still bearing traces of her baby-coat, was swollen and had been punctured by buckshot in a tightly grouped pattern. The grass all around had been flattened by her final struggles; her lips were drawn back in a snarl of pain hurled at the last cruel agonies of a lingering death.

Where was the tiger? Was he, too, either dead or dying of wounds somewhere near the cave? It was not unlikely. The cubs would almost certainly have been met together, and if they had been met with dazzling headlights, the glare would have 'fixed' them long enough for the second barrel. I searched until dark but couldn't find him.

Early the next morning I knew that he was not dead. He had drunk at the pool during the night, and when I saw the vultures keeping to the trees, I knew that he was lying somewhere close to the dead tigress.

Soon after lunch, I was up in the chair above the pool. The day was warm enough to send the tiger to drink early. But in case he was late, I had mounted a torch on a rifle. Yes, I was going to break the no-shooting-from-the-chair rule if he showed any signs of a wound serious enough either to kill him after days of agony or leave him so crippled that his life would be a misery and perhaps a danger to man and beast.

The afternoon was indeed hot and drowsy and I am ashamed to admit that the droning jungle soon lulled me to sleep. It was five-thirty before I finally struggled out of warm hazy dreams and with a sudden start saw the tiger on the far side of the water.

Fortunately, he missed the startled movement as I woke for he was looking away as he lay on the sand by the water's edge. When the sleep was off my eyes I saw that he was staring intently at a leaf blowing over the surface and drifting towards him. When it came within reach he started to dab at it with his right front paw, but with a touch so gentle that his pad was the merest caress on the tiny tip of its curled-up tail. From that moment, I always called him the Lonely Tiger. His expression was so forlorn that there flashed into my mind the vision of a small boy pondering the cruel fate that had killed first his mother and then his sister, and so condemned him to the heartache of loneliness and unexciting games played on his own.

All at once he smashed his little boat into the water with a sudden splash. *Just a silly kid's game!* Then before I quite realized what he was doing, he had reminded me why I was at the pool by starting to lick at his left front paw. From my perch thirty feet above him I saw it at once: a small patch of red flesh licked clean of fur. I leant forward to watch. But he licked nowhere else so that seemed the only wound he had. I wondered whether it would be just a single pellet from the second barrel.

I waited till he got to his feet and started down the nullah. He went slowly and with a limp, but the wound in his paw still seemed to be the only injury he had. I let him go; from that he would recover with few or no ill effects.

He was to limp for the rest of his life. On wet sand and damp earth which held the impressions of pug marks well, the left front paw always showed a little twisted with the outside toe pressing deeper than the others. This was to tell me in the years to come when the Lonely Tiger had been round.

The tiger never used the cave again and many months passed without a sign of him. Then he came back, but now he was only a casual caller because he had settled down on a regular 'beat', which took him about ten days to get round. The wound in his paw evidently had healed well and he seemed a normal tiger living on jungle game, for no report of a cattle-kill ever came in when he was about.

Some time later, he disappeared completely for nearly a year. Where he went I never knew, but it was most likely a wife that kept him away from his old haunts; when they finally called him back, he probably left a family in some distant jungle.

When at last that familiar pug mark appeared in the nullah again, it was like an unexpected visiting card from an old friend. Once more he had come back to settle down on a beat, so whenever he was expected I started to sit over the pool for I badly wanted to see what he looked like now.

He came at last on a night when there was no moon. But even a tiger cannot pass silently over dry leaves and I heard him crunching across the thick carpet of them I had spread on the nullah bed. When the torch flicked on he stopped dead and stared back at the beam. He was a magnificent animal, his coat glossy and but lightly marked with stripes. The light held him for more than a minute before he started to edge away. That night I should have taught him a lesson, a shot near his nose then might have given this story a different ending. But neither I nor the Lonely Tiger knew then that the sands of his life were running out and that he had only eight more days to live...

For the past two weeks, I had been hearing a great deal about the man shooting in the block a few miles to the north. 'One of the richest men of all, sahib,' Bhutu told me. Certainly something unusual was going on. From all accounts the camp arrangements were fantastic: luxuries galore and enough servants to astonish an old-time Viceroy. But in spite of the luxuries, hundreds of beaters, and a dozen or more young buffaloes for baits, no tiger had been shot up to the beginning of the third week.

I thought I knew what was going on. Since Independence, there have sprung up in India firms to deal with visiting sportsmen from overseas. A few of these are excellent and they do their clients well; they also observe all the forest rules and make sure that animals are shot by fair means. There are other firms not so good and some that should not be allowed to operate at all. These last ones are interested in nothing but money and if they know the forest rules they seldom obey them; and as their hunting experience is usually nil, their safest bet to get trophies is to allow their clients to shoot from jeeps.

The camp I had been hearing about was a show run by perhaps the worst of the bad firms. When this shoot was nearing its end, I happened to meet the client casually one day on the road. He hailed from some country 'south of the border' and spoke English with a strong American accent. He was very disgruntled about no tiger, for he had just come from Africa where animals 'grow on every bush'. On parting he asked me if I could sell him a tiger skin, in the event of his shoot ending with no tiger in the bag.

But the shoot was not yet over. If it had started slowly, this probably was only because the man in charge of it had no intention of making things appear too easy. He had charged a great deal of money, and it was therefore, necessary at first to make some show of getting a tiger by normal hunting methods. From what I heard the attempts had been pretty pathetic; so now, with the shoot drawing to an end, it was time to start using the jeeps at night.

They got him on the fourth night. The jeep had left camp soon after midnight for the best time was 'towards morning'. On this trip tiger again was top priority, but if anything else showed up it was not to be neglected. Nor was it. Twenty minutes after the start, an immature sambur stag fell to a .375 magnum. It was covered with leaves and left where it dropped to be collected in the morning for it was too early yet to clutter the rack at the back of the jeep: 'You just never could tell when you might want the room.' Wise counsel as it turned out, for later the rack held a chital hind.

By now time was getting on. But the night was not yet over, and just a little farther along the road another victim was waiting. As the first fingers of dawn reached up for the sky, his brilliant eyes blazed back at the headlights. For a few seconds the animal was indistinct.

Then the jeep was juddering to a crawl as the guide pointed excitedly ahead with *There he is!*

A tiger stood across the road. As the jeep purred nearer, it sounded no note of danger. His puckered mask held only a puzzled expression as the bright eyes stared at the oncoming lights. The jeep closed to a few yards. The tiger at last turned slowly towards the side of the road. As he moved, the bullet smacked into his belly, low and far back.

The tearing pain of the bullet kept him moving for almost a mile. Then the shock brought him down beside a patch of thorns. He was mortally wounded and in terrible agony. Left alone he would have gone no farther; but the first grey of dawn had now changed to lemon-coloured light and through it he saw two men, still some distance away, moving along his trail. He staggered away without being seen and then rested again where the jungle borders Bhutu's field on the northern boundary of the estate.

At dawn that morning, I was not far away from this boundary with Bhutu and two other men helping to stamp out the last smouldering patches of a fire which had burnt all night. We heard Bhutu's wife shouting long before she reached us with the news that a tiger had just crossed their field and had growled when it saw her.

We found the two men first. They were examining a fresh patch of blood under a tree. One was armed with an old single barrel 12-bore, the other had an axe. When I had found out who they were, they readily told the whole story and then amazed me more by explaining how they had been left behind 'to find the dead tiger'. The rest, with One-Shot Sam, had gone comfortably home to a hearty breakfast.

When the men were forbidden to search farther, the one with the gun started to argue. The tiger, he said, had to be found. The foreign burra sahib badly wanted the skin and would make trouble if he didn't get it. I sent Bhutu and Jaganath to see them on their way and to make sure that they did not slip back.

When I started to follow the blood trail, I was still unaware that I was after the Lonely Tiger. He ought to have been miles away on his beat for he was not due back for another two or three days. But where the trail left the leafy carpet of the forest for a path through scrub, I suddenly found that twisted pug clearly printed in the fine dust. This, although a shock, was also a help. A strange tiger would have been making off at random and any cover that offered the slightest security might have concealed it. But not this one. At least I was ready to bet that when thinking of a safe place to hide he would be making for the cave.

The trail was easy to follow. The tiger, still losing blood, had kept to a path which winds diagonally across the side of a wooded hill. Near the bottom of this the path forks, the right branch curling down to the nullah, the other going on over boulder-strewn ground under heavy jungle to the tiger's old cave. The blood turned away to the right. My guess had been wrong, but once that idea had been tossed out of my mind I realized that the pool in the nullah was the obvious place for the tiger to make for. What he must need now more than anything else was water.

I should find him by the pool. That was certain; for he had been forced to rest at two places on the way down from the top of the hill and that had slowed him up considerably; now, he could not be very far ahead. From the fork, I crept to within fifty yards of the nullah and then left the path to make a detour through the jungle, which would bring me out above the pool from a flank.

I regretted doing this at once. The noise of my progress now was dangerous. The surface of the path had been powder-soft and dead silent, but the ground here was strewn with dry leaves and I seemed to be treading on them all. There was no time to go back. Having once started it was best to keep going as quietly as I could and make for a screen of bushes ahead that edged the bank just above the pool. At last I reached them and paused briefly; then I inched forward the last two yards and looked down at the pool.

The nullah bed was empty. One quick sweeping glance took it all in. Then a sudden chill swept through me when I saw what I had walked into. The water in the pool was cloudy with slow swirls of muddy sediment still settling to the bottom. The tiger had only just left. Across the dry sand, I could see the deep pocks left by his pugs still ringed with a thin wet line. The tracks led from the water to where the path sloped up the bank…the path I had just left.

There could be little doubt that he had heard me coming. But now, instead of running away, he had turned to meet the threat and had come up the path to fight. From somewhere very close he was watching me. I kept quite still, ears straining, eyes searching frantically for some sign: the attack might come at any second—the only warning a sudden noisy charge over the dry leaves from wherever he was hiding.

I saw him first from the corner of my eye. He was crouched by a teak tree twenty yards off and a little behind me. The next second, the foresight was racing towards him.

But I was too late. Death was staring straight back at me from the tiger's eyes even as I swung towards him. As I stared back, I heard the pounding of my heart and the frantic cries of monkeys which had just spotted him from the trees along the nullah. They were very excited. But then they didn't know as I did that the Lonely Tiger was dead.

The Kharakpoor Hills

EDWARD LOCKWOOD

Twenty years ago anyone standing on the summit of the hills adjoining Kharakpoor, would have been surrounded by a dense and almost impenetrable forest, where, at sunrise peacocks and jungle-fowl were heard calling to their mates, and where in the evening tigers, leopards and bears, came to drink the water of the little river Mun, which, rising at the hot springs in the recesses of the hills, flowed, forming many beautiful cascades by the way, between the hills, until it reached the plains near Kharakpoor. The past twenty years, however, have effected greater changes in these hills than did the twenty centuries which had gone before. Directly the railway whistle was heard on the adjoining loop-line of the East India Railway, the wild animals retired to happier hunting grounds; the peacocks and jungle-fowl followed, and soon the forest, resounding with the woodman's axe, gave way to fields of wheat,

Essay taken from: Lockwood, Edward. *Natural History, Sport and Travel* (London: William H. Allen and Co., 1878), pp. 107–22.

cotton, sessamum and other fertile crops, such as may only be seen in India on virgin soil.

Nor are these the only changes which have taken place. The little river Mun can no longer sing as it goes along—

> 'For men may come and men may go,
> But I flow on for ever.'

because the narrow gorge through which it passed on its way to Kharakpoor has been closed, and its collected waters form one of the most lovely lakes in the world, rivalling, by no mere figure of speech, the renowned lakes of Killamey.

This great engineering work, which has been carried out at a cost of some lakhs of rupees, debited to the Darbhanga Raj, sets a drought through the surrounding country at defiance, and will enable the happy rayat to raise a succession of crops all the year round. As the lake is as yet in its infancy, being only a few months old, the number of European visitors who have seen its beauties may be counted on the fingers; and on January 1, the first picnic took place upon its banks, which assuredly, before long, will resound with the voices of pleasure-parties and tourists.

Our party consisted of myself and my wife, Major Waller, the District Superintendent of Police, and Mrs Waller, the Assistant Magistrate Mr Primrose, and Mr King, the officer in charge of the Kharakpoor estate. Our intention being to combine business with pleasure, and explore the lake, following the course of the stream as far as possible among the hills.

On our arrival at the lake, we found a jolly boat, manned by four rowers, waiting for us; and, whilst its prow was being decked with a garland of flowers, in order, as the boatmen assured us, to procure a propitious voyage, we examined the trees and plants which grew on the neighbouring hill-side down to the water's edge. Here we found beautiful blue and pink Barlerias growing side by side with the gaudy yellow wood-cotton flower (Hibiscus vitifolius), and with them the pink Amaranthus, with seed vessels like miniature Burmese boxes, and a pale blue Eranthemum, which quite deserves a place in the flower-garden. Towering above these were *Wrightia tinctoria*, with its curious follicles or pods, like miniature horse-collars. The Indian Olax, which my companions at once pronounced to be an oak, because the fruit closely resembles an acorn; the Jungle Crab (*Zizyphus xylopyra*), and the spreading *Woodfordia floribunda*, which maybe called a country cousin of the cultivated pomegranate. Over these was creeping in beautiful profusion the Silver Creeper (*Porana paniculata*), known to Europeans as 'the bride', but by a curious perversion of terms, the 'boori', or old woman, by the natives, who seem unable to distinguish what is sweet and fair, from what is old and ugly.

We were assisted into the boat by a fine soldierly looking Sikh orderly, belonging to the Court of Wards, who asked us what chance there was of war with Russia, adding that directly the war-note sounded, we might count on him to bring one man and horse into the field. He confided to us that he had a natural taste for fighting, and. that fighting in company with Englishmen was the summit of his ambition.

Directly the boat started, the beauties of the lake began to unfold themselves. On one side range after range of hills arose, until they were crowned by the table-topped Marak, over one thousand five hundred feet high, which makes a most conspicuous landmark; whilst on the other hand were abrupt precipices, with gigantic boulders piled together, forming a fine eyrie to a horned rock owl, which, unaccustomed to visitors in his highland home, greeted us, as long as we remained in sight, with cries of 'Who? *Who?*'

Twenty minutes pull brought us to what formerly was known as the Fakir's Cave. This was a small chamber in the overhanging rocks, some thirty feet above the stream, where a mendicant, for reasons best known to himself, had taken up his abode for many years, until— so the simple people say—a goddess, in the shape of a tiger, claimed him for her own. The great attraction to the place was a huge sacred tree, a Terminalia, said to be the habitation of the goddess; and the woodmen had built her a temple on the other side of the stream. Both the temple and the cave are now deep beneath the lake, and the goddess appears to have assumed the form of a parakeet, for we saw numbers of these birds building their nests in the cavities of the sacred tree, now devoid of leaves, and up to its waist in water. The lake is narrow here, as the cliffs on either side close up, only to stretch out again further on, and a drum beaten, or a gun fired, re-echoes again and again among the rocks, until the sound dies away among the distant hills.

The place is full of interest, particularly to those who can compare it now with what it was a year ago.

A little further on last year, I visited a cascade, known by the name of the Fountain of the Seven Sisters, and I found monkeys clambering over the rocks forty feet above my head. These rocks now appear beneath the water as we sit above them in the boat, and the cascade has disappeared for ever.

A similar fate lias befallen the 'Laughing Fountain' higher up, where the water was said to be the sweetest in all the country round; and a huge banyan with its numerous slender roots and trunks close by standing out of the water, affords a fine look out to an Egyptian vulture and Indian snake-bird (*Plotus melanogaster*), which have taken possession of it.

Where the banks are low, and there is any level land, clearings have been made, and the Santhal rayats came running up to see us as we passed, and hearing the sound of the dram, showed a strong disposition to commence a dance in honour of our arrival. Yirgil's line, which commences 'O *fortunati nimium*', may be translated, in order to apply to them, 'O, happy race! if you would only keep from drink.' They hold their lands at very low rates, and with ordinary care, they might soon become rich, but they are an improvident people, and appear doomed to extinction. We have now been rowing for two hours, and have come nearly seven miles. The stream begins to narrow up, and the coxswain finds difficulty in avoiding the trunks of the trees standing in the water, so, choosing a clear place, where the banks are not too high to land, we direct the boat to shore, and, as it strikes the bushes overhanging the water, we disturb three otters, which greet us with terrified stares, and plunge into the water. On the beat of our drum Santhals peep out of the bushes, like the Sherwood foresters, when the Black Knight sounded his horn; and under the promise of largesse, their services are retained to collect wood for a fire, and to serve as guides to those of our party who wish to explore the woods, and collect plants and ferns.

We felt as we sat at breakfast under a large frankincense tree, that if this, the first picnic which has taken place on the Kharakpoor lake were a fail sample of Indian life, there would be very little to grumble at in India, either as regards the scenery or the climate.

I was never tired of collecting specimens of natural history among the hills, for prizes turned up at almost every step, and my companions were always so glad to hear about the plants and birds and insects which we saw around, that I sometimes doubted the wisdom of the English system of education, which leaves so little time for the study of natural history.

Over our heads as we sat at breakfast a colony of Blue-tailed Bee-eaters (*Merops philippensis*) were breakfasting on flies. These birds are hardly distinguishable when on the wing from the *Merops apiaster* of Europe, and which is so unfavourably spoken of in the fourth Georgic. They form large colonies in Monghyr, on the banks of the Ganges, where I often found their eggs. The holes which they inhabit are frequently attacked by bull-frogs, which eat the young birds or eggs. The old birds, too, are also killed when the frogs can catch them, and my attention was once called to a huge bull-frog with a Mynah (*Acridotheres tristis*) struggling in its mouth. The pretty little Green Bee-eater (*Merops viridis*) is also present. Several are sitting without any fear on a bush close by, and darting down on mosquitoes, which are hastening by scores from the water to annoy us. These birds also breed in colonies near Monghyr. I have found their eggs in holes of banks hardly a foot high, and which appear like the habitations of rats rather than of birds.

If the beauty of flowers is due to natural selection, that creative power has not been very active here, for gaudy flowers are conspicuous by their absence. An honourable exception, however, may be made of what is locally known as the Nepal lilac, a member of the *Cinchona* family (*Hamiltonia suaveolens*), whose fragrant flowers scent the air around. Another exception is the Myrtle-flowered Styrax (*Symplocos spicata*), which called forth much admiration from our party, as it grew in great luxuriance by the water-side. The capsules of yams hung clustering overhead, and reminded us of the Bryony of English hedgerows. I sent a large collection of the various wild yams, which the poor foresters eat in Monghyr, to the Economic Museum in Calcutta. They were collected by Major Waller, the District Superintendent of Police, during his cold weather tour among the hills.

The water's edge, where our boat is anchored, is yellow with the Indian ranunculus, the only member of the butter-cup family which I have noticed in Monghyr; and the gum-arabic tree close by is also covered with yellow threads, which look as though a net had been thrown over it to preserve the precious gum from the attacks of birds.

The net is the silken parasite, *Cassyta filiformis*, which always attracts the attention of travellers in Monghyr; and hundreds of orange-tipped butterflies (*Ixias marianne*) are hovering over it.

As we are making our way through the bushes after breakfast, in search of birds and plants, our guide screamed out 'Sai!' 'Sai!'*

---

* Hindustani for porcupine.

and a porcupine dashed by, which Mr Primrose knocked over with a ball. The Santhal gave a yell of delight, and begged the body for a feast; so after extracting a few quills as a momento of the day, we made the Santhal happy, and Prisoner-of-Chillon-like in the evening when we let him go—

'He regained his freedom with a sai.'

But not only are flowers scarce in the primeval forests, but birds and beasts are rare. We saw a solitary crested hawk-eagle perched on a leafless tree, and a few parakeets flew screaming by. The lake has not yet been discovered by the myriads of wild fowl which pass over Monghyr; but we saw a flamingo, evidently a straggler, cooling his long legs in the water which washed the shore.

A few cormorants have taken up their quarters here, attracted by the fish, and the white-breasted kingfisher (*Halcyon smyrnensis*), the pied kingfisher (*Ceryle rudis*), and the little blue kingfisher (*Alcedo bengalensis*), breed in great security on the steep banks along the stream. The water will doubtless soon be full of fish, and as the stream before it was dammed up, was the home of the far-famed Mahseer (*Barbus tor*). These should now attain gigantic size, and afford good sport to the angler. There is also a curious little fish, which may be called the river remora (*Discognathus lamta*), for nature has provided it with a sucker beneath its jaws, which enables it to attach itself to the rocks and resist the terrific current to which it was exposed during the rainy season, when the Mun was only a mountain stream. Now, in the still waters of the lake, the sucker is no longer required, and according to the evolution theory it will disappear. Here, too, is the home of a goby (*G. giuris*), whose ventral fins also form a disc, and enable it to fasten itself to rocks, and resist the force of sudden floods when they come down from the hills. At least a dozen species of carp are common, and a beaked gar-fish (*Belone cancila*), locally known as the cowal. Unfortunately a pair of crocodiles have taken tip their abode in the lake, and will make sad havoc among the fish. But reptiles are scarce among the hills. The only snake we saw was the yellow-collared green snake (*Tropidonotus plumbicolor*). Although perfectly harmless, it is declared to be very venomous by the natives, who say it flies. Two or three species of skinks we found running about the rocks; and these, though quite harmless, have a bad name among the natives.

By the time we had collected specimens of all the plants we could find, and the artist of the party had filled his book with sketches, the sun threw long shadows from the distant purple hills, and we saw the horned rock-owl flying across the lake, previous to commencing his hunting for the night. Night-jars also crept out of the brushwood, where they had been taking their siesta in the shade. The painted spur-fowls, thinking the coast was clear, were coming down to drink, and as we passed they witnessed the termination of the first picnic on the beautiful lake at Kharakpoor.

Next day we visited Bhim-band, some twenty miles up the river Mun, where several hot springs rise out of the rocks side by side, with a spring of pure cold water, which supplies most of the water to the lake. The temperature of the hot springs is 140 degrees, similar to the Sitakund fountain at Monghyr. But Bhim-band is not a place of pilgrimage now, as it was in the old days, being deep in the recesses of the jungle, and anyone who visits it, must take a guide to show the way through the unfrequented forest paths. A thakur, or holy man, who holds the land around, has evidently an eye for the picturesque, and will not allow the forest trees about his hermitage to be cut. We found some splendid specimens of the banyan, the silk-cotton tree (*Bombax*), the mahwa (*Bassea latifolia*), and a bignonia with long pods (*Steresospermum suaveolens*), which we had not seen before. It is a paradise for botanists, and the huge basket which we carried was soon full with specimens of at least fifty species of forest trees. Here we also saw, flying overhead with a speed which the eye can hardly follow, the graceful crested swift (*Dendrochelidon coronatus*), only to be found in the deep recesses of the hills; and the wild cry of hornbills was heard on all sides. These birds, which, we were told, breed in the hollow trees around, get very fat on the numerous berries in the woods at this season of the year; and they share the wild plums with the few bears which have hitherto escaped affording the Government reward for their skins to the hunters, who are ever on the watch.

The tigers, for which the neighbourhood of the hot springs was famed only a few years back, have now nearly all disappeared; but not long ago our friend, the thakur, was cutting wood near his home when a tiger sprang out, seized his servant who was with him, and was carrying him off to the jungle, when the thakur attacked the tiger with his walking-stick, and so astonished the brute that he dropped his victim unhurt, and made off into the woods. We asked this brave and holy man before we left, what he knew of the outside world; but he appeared never to have heard of the Empress of India, or her royal son, and his visit to India. He declared that all knowledge of rulers, beyond myself, who paid him a yearly visit, was a blank. Here was a contented man, an Indian Rasselas, living among the Kharakpoor hills; and more than one of our party, as we wished the holy man good-bye, and retraced our steps towards home and work, declared such a life was to be envied. And on asking him, the thakur said, and probably truly, that he had no desire to change places with us, even if he could, notwithstanding that he viewed us in the light of the kings of the country. His rude ideas on the subject are elegantly expressed in Goldsmith's, or rather Johnson's lines—

> 'The lifted axe, the agonizing wheel,
> Luke's iron crown, and Damien's bed of steel,
> To men remote from power but rarely known,
> Leave virtue, faith and conscience all our own.'

The Seven Sisters

FRANK FINN

'*We are seven.*'—Wordsworth.

S ome years back, a new Viceroy was being shown the wonders of his temporary kingdom, and among these the Taj at Agra held, of course, an important place. Arrived before the glorious monument of Eastern love and pride, 'the artless Aide-de-Camp was mute; the gilded staff were still' as Kipling says, in anxious expectation of the comment of His Excellency. But this, alas! when it came was merely the remark: 'What are those funny little birds?' The shock must have been the greater for the fact that the mean fowls thus honoured were it seems, of that singularly disreputable species which is commonly known in India as the 'Seven Sisters' or 'Seven Brothers', or by the Hindustani equivalent of *sat-bhai*. In books it gets called the Jungle Babbler, the first part of the name being inappropriate, for it is found everywhere, and the last singularly happy, for it does babble with a vengeance. As may be inferred from their popular names, these

Essay taken from: Finn, Frank. *The Birds of Calcutta*, second edition (Calcutta: Thacker, Spink & Co., 1904), pp. 15–21.

birds go about in small packs of about half-a-dozen—there are not invariably seven, nor can these be a family party, since only three or four eggs are laid. They hop about searching for food on the ground or branches, murmuring squeakily to themselves meanwhile, and ever and anon burst out into a startling volley of wheezy hysterical chatter, which gets terribly upon one's nerves in time in a place where they are common. Linnaeus, when he called the bird *Turdus canorus*, the tuneful thrush, must have been wildly ignorant of it, or have hopelessly mixed it up with an ally and a real songster, the huamei of China (*Trochalopterum canorum*), which he included under the same name. Modern ornithologists call our babbling brotherhood *Crateropus canorus*, placing them in a different family from the true thrushes, to which they nevertheless bear a strong general resemblance in form and size. But the differences are very soon perceptible if one studies the living birds. Your thrush is sleek, stiff, and starch; he is a musical artist, but allows himself no artistic license in his dress, which is neat to primness. The Babblers, on the contrary, have a fluffy, frowsy appearance; their tails hang loosely, and their wings, which are short, are not neatly tucked up as they should be, but lie anyhow. Nor have they the excuse of pleasing colour, such as many clumsy birds can boast of; a brownish grey, of 'unparalleled dignitude' as Baboo Jabberjee would say, is almost the only hue visible in their attire, and is not particularly well set off by a white eye like a jackdaw's and whitish legs and bill of an unpleasantly anaemic appearance. There is, however, a real interest attaching to these disreputable-looking birds. We are all familiar with Lamb's appallingly ugly lady whose facial turpitude was supposed to be atoned for by the possession of superlative moral excellence; and unquestionably fraternal affection is the strong point of the babbling brotherhood. In the grave pages of the Asiatic Society's Journal a friend of mine has recorded his frequent experience of the devoted courage with which these feeble-winged creatures will rush to the defence of a comrade held in the grip of a trained hawk—on one occasion the victim was actually rescued by its comrades before the hawk could receive its master's assistance, and on another, one of the Babblers was caught by hand as it clung to the back of its relative's murderer. No one, so far as I am aware, has recorded behaviour anything like this on the part of our song-thrush (Turdus musicus), who appears to be rather a coward, although his near relative the missel-thrush (Turdus viscivorus) will show fight boldly in defence of his home and mate. And with regard to these Babblers courage appears to be a variable quality even in this particular species; for Dr Jerdon expressly states that the Jungle Babbler will not attack a trained hawk flown at the flock as the bolder Mahratta Babbler (Argya malcolmi) will. Dehra Dun, therefore, where the above incident occurred, must be inhabited by a peculiarly warlike clan of Crateropus canorus, and certainly they are very numerous there and obtrusively noisy. That sociability is a passion with the species no one who has studied it can doubt; I have kept several, and have found that they almost invariably exhibited the spirit of the poet's goldfinch, who—

'A prison with a friend preferred
To liberty without.'

If one found himself outside the cage which contained the happy family, he 'did his possible' to get in again without any thought of escape. It may be ungenerously suggested that such birds are afraid to go about alone, lest their ribald remarks, made in the security of numbers, meet with a just retaliation at the beaks and claws of outraged bird society; and so it may be, but nevertheless there is a well-spring of sincere sociability under the Babbler's frowsy feathering. On the comparatively rare occasions when my captives were still, they employed themselves in affectionately tickling each other's heads as they cuddled together, and I have even seen one diligently employed in endeavouring to clean the wing of a friend, soiled by the bird lime with which its capture had been effected. At the same time it must be admitted that the addition to their ordinary diet of table scraps of such a delicacy as a cockroach was apt to produce a sad disruption of fraternal harmony. On such occasions one might see one brother prone in the sand, while another, holding his head 'in chancery' with one foot, was punching the same with his beak in a manner calculated to awake grave fears for the integrity of the sufferer's skull when the punishment should be over; and once I saw two birds adherent with bill and claw to one and the same cockroach, which a third was devouring, as neither of the joint owners dared to let go his hold! These traits of character would seem to show that *Crateropus canorus* is in about the same stage of moral evolution as that represented by the public school boy, a gallant defender of his kind against the assaults of 'cads', 'nippers' and 'vulgar plebs' generally, but inclined also to be severe on them in individual disputes.

The reason for the development of such clannishness is obvious when the very weak flight of this bird is noticed; the short wings are beaten quickly for a short distance, and the labour is economised by a gliding skim till a fresh effort is required and with such a method of flight escape by aerial evolutions is very much at a discount. On his feet the Babbler is much more at home, and hops along with considerable speed, never running smoothly as the true thrushes often do. He differs from these birds also in another noticeable point in the use of the feet, having the crow-like habit of using them to hold anything large he is eating—a thing no thrush would stoop to do—or think of doing, more likely. Babblers also resemble crows and differ from most thrushes in the young birds being like their parents; young thrushes being, as everyone knows, much more spotted than old ones. Whether the Babblers go through any elaborate courtship ceremony I cannot say; male and female are equally ugly, but this does not prevent some birds from making themselves ridiculous before the object of their affections, and possibly these are among the number—a Babbler could not be dignified if he tried. Their nest is just about the sort of abode one would expect them to build, a simple cup, more or less loose and untidy, placed almost anywhere in shrubs or trees. But the eggs are the one beautiful thing about the bird, being of that lovely blue so noticeable in the hedge-sparrow's at home, and very glossy in addition. As above implied the young ones fledge oft very like the old, but they have dark brown instead of white eyes. A very plump one I experimentally ate tasted much like a quail, and herein perhaps lies an economic possibility for the 'Seven Sisters'; clan would just about fill a pie. The French in Algeria regard the local babbler there (*Argya fulva*) as *gibier*, but their notions in that matter are known to be liberal; witness the colonists in New Caledonia who used to eat the local crow, until one day a native asked one of these sportsmen why the white men ate what they religiously avoided, giving as a reason, when questioned, that the said crows ate them when exposed dead on platforms in the forest according to custom. After this crow ceased to figure in the Colonial menu.

The said Algerian Babbler is the nearest of the family to Europe, and generally speaking, babblers inhabit Africa and the Oriental region only. Our familiar suburban friend, which is found all over India, is the only one about here in a wild state, though several of his more or less close relatives may be met with at bird-dealer's places, including the above mentioned huamei of China, recognizable by its russet plumage and white eyebrows, and another species common to that country and Farther India, the slate-coloured, white-cheeked Chinese mocking-bird or peko (*Dryonastes chinensis*), which, though obviously of the vulgar babbler family, is a finer songster than almost any bird I have heard, and a mocker to boot. Some day, possibly, when people begin to realize that desirable birds can be cultivated in gardens as well as desirable plants (the efforts of humanity in the former direction hitherto having been largely expended in the acclimatization of nuisances) we may have the peko making our gardens melodious and supplanting the 'shrieking sisterhood' altogether—a consummation devoutly to be wished, although, till some such better bird takes their place, their industriously insectivorous habits may give, them a *raison d'être*.

The Indian Leopard

RICHARD LYDEKKER

NATIVE NAMES.—*Chita, Sona-chita, Chita-bagh, Adnara,* AND *Tendwa,* HINDUSTANI; *Palang,* PERSIAN; *Diho,* BALUCHI; *Suh,* KASHMIRI; *Tidua* AND *Srighas* IN BUNDELKAND; *Gorbacha* OR *Borbacha,* DECCANI; *Karda, Asnea, Singhal* AND *Bibia-bagh,* MAHRATHI; *Tenderwa* AND *Bibla* AMONG THE BAURIS OF THE DECCAN; *Honiga* AND *Kerkal,* CANARESE; *Teon-kula* OF THE KOLS; *Jerkos* AMONG THE RAJMEHAL HILL-TRIBES; *Burkal* AND *Gordag* OF THE GONDS; *Sonora* OF THE KORKUS; *Chiru-thai,* TAMIL; *Chinna-pali,* TELEGU; *Pali,* MALABARI; *Kutiya,* CINGALESE; *Bai-hira, Tehr-he, Goral-he* OR *Ghor-he* OF THE HILL-TRIBES OF THE SIMLA DISTRICT; *Sik,* TIBETAN; *Syik, Syiak* OR *Sejjiak* OF THE LEPCHAS; *Kajengla,* MANIPURI; *Misi-patrai* AND *Kam-kei* OF THE KUKIS OF THE MISHMI HILLS; *Hurrea-kon, Morrh, Rusa, Tekhu-Khuia* AND *Kekhi* OF THE NAGAS; *Kya-lak* OR *Kya-thit,* BURMESE; *Klapreung,* TALAIN; *Kiche-phong* OF THE KARENS; *Rimau-bintang,* MALAY

Essay taken from: Lydekkar, Richard. *The Great and Small Game of India, Burma and Tibet* (London: Rowland Ward Limited, 1900), pp. 292–305.

A mong the numerous instances of confusion and uncertainty as to the proper application and signification of names in natural history, perhaps no greater 'muddle' exists than in the case of the large spotted cat whose scientific title is undoubtedly *Felis pardus*. As is stated in the article 'Leopard' in the ninth edition of the *Encyclopedia Britannica*, as well as in Mr R.A. Sterndale's *Natural History of Indian Mammalia*, this animal was known to the ancients by the names of *pardalis* and *panthera*, which subsequently became Anglicised into pard and panther. At the same early date the animal now known as the hunting-leopard was designated *leopardus*, or leopard, from the idea that it was a hybrid between the lion and the pard. As time went on, the name 'pard' gradually fell into disuse, and the term leopard became transferred from the animal to which it originally belonged to one of the varieties of *Felis pardus*, panther being, however, still retained for another form of the same animal, on the supposition that there were two distinct species of these spotted cats.

This transference of the name leopard to *Felis pardus* left the animal to which it originally pertained without a popular title of any kind. Accordingly, the Hindustani name chita (meaning spotted or speckled) was made to do duty for the animal in question. Such a restriction is, however, quite unjustifiable, for although by the natives of India the latter title is applied indifferently to *Felis pardus* and *Cynalurus jubatus*,* in almost ninety-nine out of every hundred occasions on which it is employed, the former animal will be the one designated. Sometimes, indeed, it may happen that if a native of India wishes to particularise the exact kind of chita to which he may be referring, he will distinguish *Felis pardus* either as sona-chita (golden chita), or as chita-bagh (spotted tiger), but on nearly all occasions chita suffices.

---

* To avoid hopeless confusion in this connection, it is a almost essential to use the scientific names of the two animals.

The best way out of the double difficulty is to drop the use of the term chita altogether, and to call *Cynalurus jubatus* the hunting-leopard, while the term leopard is assigned to *Felis pardus*.

But here another difficulty presents itself. The majority of Indian sportsmen are persuaded that, in addition to the hunting-leopard, there are two perfectly distinct species of large spotted cats, which they respectively call leopard and panther. And it is a matter for regret that the idea of the specific distinctness of the animals so designated has been supported by such a good naturalist as Mr Sterndale. It may, however, be regarded as certain that the animals in question are at most but varieties of a single species, of which they not improbably indicate a larger and a smaller race.

Accordingly, it is justifiable to use only a single English name for this species, although we may mark the occurrence of two races, if such really exist, by designating one as the lesser, and the other the larger Indian leopard, the name 'panther' being allowed to fall, so far as possible, into oblivion.

Having cleared the ground thus far, the next point is the definition of the animal it is agreed to call the leopard (*Felis pardus*). Briefly, it may be said that under this term are included all the varieties of large ring-spotted cats inhabiting the Old World, with the exception of the snow-leopard, of which the distinctive features are pointed out in the sequel. From the hunting-leopard, the present species, in addition to the difference in general bodily form and the structure of the claws, is broadly distinguished by the circumstance that a large proportion of the spots on the back and sides are in the shape of large circular broken rosettes, whereas all those of the former animal are solid and smaller. The only other cat with which the leopard is the least liable to be confounded is the jaguar of the New World, which is recognisable at a glance by the presence of a small black central spot to each rosette, of which there is no trace in the leopard.

In size the leopard, as might be expected from its wide geographical distribution, is a very variable species, the extremes of total length ranging from as little as five to as much as eight feet, or thereabouts. The general ground-colour of the upper-parts varies from olive through rufous to pale yellow or brownish yellow, and that of the under-parts from yellow to pure white. The black spots on the head and lower part of the limbs are always small and solid; and such solid spots may be continued on to the neck and shoulders, as well as in a double line down the middle of the hinder part of the back, while the greater portion of the outer surface of the limbs may occasionally be solid-spotted. Over a larger or smaller extent of the upper surface of the body and outer side of the upper portion of the limbs the spots take the form of rosettes, consisting of a black, and frequently interrupted external ring, and a pale centre, which may or may not be darker than the general ground-colour. On the underparts the spots are solid, and often lighter-coloured than those of the back, being generally also much larger and more irregularly shaped than those on the head. On the upper surface of the tail the spots are elongated and light-centred; but towards the tip of the upper surface they assume the form of broad transverse bars, the under surface of the tail-tip being uniformly yellowish or white.

Marked local differences in bodily form and in the length of the tail and hair are likewise noticeable, the Manchurian race being a much more heavily-built and longer-haired animal than the leopard of Bengal.

The distribution of the leopard is very extensive, including the greater part of Africa, Asia Minor, the Caucasus, Syria, Palestine, Persia, Baluchistan, Afghanistan, a large part of Central Asia, India, Assam, Ceylon, Burma, the Malay Peninsula, Siam, China, Manchuria, Java and Sumatra.

With this enormous geographical range, it is only natural to suppose that the leopard should be divisible into a considerable number of local races. And that this is the case may be regarded as certain, although unfortunately the specimens in our museums are at present insufficient to enable the determination and definition of such local races to be properly worked out.

The first point in connection with an investigation of this nature is to determine the locality of the typical *Felis pardus* of Linnaeus, by whom the species was originally named. In the *Systema Naturae* the first reference is to the figure of an African representative of the species, and this might at first sight be taken to indicate that the typical leopard is the African form.* But at the conclusion of his brief notice Linnaeus gives the habitat of the species as in *Indis*; and since the description speaks of all the spots on the upper surface being annulated, this accords much better with the Indian than with the African animal.

African leopards are characterised by the spots being very numerous and of comparatively small size, and more especially by the circumstance that the whole or the greater portion of those on the fore part of the body—that is to say, about as far back as the hinder side of the shoulders—are in the form of irregular solid spots, the rosettes not making their appearance till behind the shoulder-blades.** Frequently, too, these solid spots tend to continue for some distance down the middle line of the back; and the great majority, if not the whole of the spots on the limbs, are of the solid type, although larger than those on the shoulders. As a rule, the middle line of the back is marked by a broad dark streak, and the centres of the rosettes are elsewhere not conspicuously darker than the general ground-colour. In a few skins the rosettes all over the body

---

* This appears to have been the view taken by the French naturalist Temminck.

** Occasionally some of the spots in the region of the shoulders show small light centres.

tend to break up into small irregular spots. It may be added that it is occasionally difficult to decide whether a particular skin is Indian or African, although there is no difficulty at all in determining the locality of a series.

Another important point is that there are no truly black leopards in Africa. Occasionally, however, specimens are met with on the high grounds of South Africa in which practically the whole of the rosettes are broken up into minute, widely separated spots, while the ground-colour is much darker than usual and the middle line of the back almost completely black. In one such specimen the semi-blackness of the back extends over the whole of the upper parts, although the spots are still more or less distinctly visible. It may be added that African leopards appear to run comparatively small.

In East African specimens the ground-colour of the skin is generally a light golden tawny, with the under parts and the inner surfaces of the limbs white. On the other hand, leopards from the moist forest region of the west coast are very much darker, the ground-colour of the upper parts being olive-tawny, and that of the lower parts yellow-tawny.

In the year 1777 Erxleben applied the name *Felis leopardus* to the African leopard, and in the absence of any evidence to the contrary, it may perhaps be permissible to consider this form typified by the East African leopard, which should then be known (as being merely a variety of the species of which the Indian leopard is the type) as *F. pardus leopardus*. Admitting this, it next becomes a question whether the West African form should be included under the same sub-title. If we had only these two forms to deal with, the West African might certainly be separated as a distinct race. But since both forms agree in the general arrangement of their spots, and thereby differ from all the Asiatic representatives of the species, such a classification would not adequately express the relationships of the different modifications. It would, indeed, require a quadrinomial system to properly indicate such distinctions, but since this is not yet adopted in zoology, it seems better for the present to regard all the African leopards as belonging to a single race, of which the eastern form may be designated as *Felis pardus leopardus, a*, and the western as *F. pardus leopardus, b*.

Turning to Asia, it will be found that all Indian leopards have the spots larger, less numerous, and more widely separated than in the African animal, while the rosettes extend forwards on the back as far as the hinder region of the neck, and likewise reach some way down the upper region of the limbs.* In no case does the middle line of the back form such a conspicuously dark streak as in the African leopard, and in many skins there is no appreciable darkening in this region at all. Individual specimens, more especially in the Malay countries, are, however, completely black, so that the spots and rosettes are visible only in certain lights. Frequently the centres of the rosettes on the back are appreciably darker than the general ground-colour. As regards the length of the fur and the thickness of the tail, Indian and African leopards are very similar, the fur on both body and tail being short and close.

These differences are amply sufficient to justify the separation of the Indian leopard as a race apart from the African representative of the species, and as it has already been shown that the Indian leopard is the typical representative of the species, its full title will be *Felis pardus iypica*. But, as has already been indicated, Indian leopards are by no means all precisely alike (although differing in all the above features from their African relative), sportsmen recognising a larger form, which they call panther, and a smaller one, to which they restrict the title leopard. It appears that the lesser Indian leopard, which is the one generally met with in the plains of Peninsular India,

---

* These features are well shown in the figures of Chinese leopard skins on pp. 16 and 17 of Dr Bonavia's *Studies in the Evolution of Animals*.

is characterised by the relatively small size of the rosettes, the pale tint of the ground-colour, and the absence of darkening in the central area of the rosettes, these features being generally accompanied by a greater length of tail and a shorter head. On the other hand, in the larger Indian leopard, which is generally found in the damp forest regions of Bengal, Assam, the Terai, Burma and probably the Malay countries, the ground-colour of the fur tends to reddish, the central areas of the rosettes are darker than the rest of the fur, and the tail is relatively short and the head long. A mounted example of this form is exhibited, in a crouching attitude, in the British Museum. Although in a large series of specimens it may be difficult to assign individual skins and skulls to one or the other, if the two forms are, as a whole, distinguishable and restricted to particular localities, they are undoubtedly entitled to recognition. But in view of what has been said with regard to the two colour-phases of the African leopard, there are inconveniences in the way of regarding them as races. Accordingly, it is proposed to include them both under the title of *Felis pardus typica*, taking the larger form, which may be designated *a*, as the type of that race, and distinguishing the smaller animal as *b*. The above-mentioned mounted specimen may be taken as a typical representative of the larger form of the Indian race, and therefore of the species.

The Indian leopard, as already mentioned, probably extends into the Malay countries and the south of China. In Baluchistan, Persia, etc., it is replaced by a distinct race, of which the characteristics are given under a separate heading. In Manchuria the species is represented by an extremely different race (*F. pardus fontanieri*), which presents features analogous to those of the Manchurian tiger, as compared with its Bengal relative. The Manchurian leopard, of which a fine mounted example is exhibited in the British Museum, is much more distinct than either of the other local races of the species, presenting, indeed, the extreme of divergence from the small-spotted African race.

In its general massiveness of build the Manchurian leopard is indeed very similar to the tiger of the same region, having stout and somewhat clumsy limbs, a relatively short and broad head, and long and thick fur.

Another analogy to the Manchurian tiger is presented by the type of coloration, the spots being very much larger and more widely separated from one another than is the case with the Indian leopard. The ground-colour of the fur is very pale sandy, but the light centres of the rosettes, especially on the back, are very much darker than the general body-colour. The solid spots of the head are continued on to the region of the shoulders, and thence down the whole of the fore-limbs, similar solid spots reappearing on the hind-legs. These large spots are widely separated from one another, and nearly circular in shape, and are thus markedly different from the small, closely-crowded, and irregular solid spots on the fore-quarters of the African leopard, while they are equally different from the annulated spots occurring in the same region of the Indian race of the species. The dark rings are, in fact, much less broken up than in either the Indian or the African race. A leopard skin from Shensi, Northern China, recently presented to the British Museum by Father Hugh, seems to be intermediate between the Manchurian and large Indian race. It has the long hair and thick tail of the former, but resembles the latter in the rich tawny ground-colour of the fur, and also in the prevalence of rosettes, especially on the hind-quarters.

Black leopards, it may be observed, are not entitled to be regarded as a distinct race, being only specially coloured individuals of the larger Indian leopard, which, as already mentioned, is the form found not only in Bengal but apparently also in Burma and the Malay countries. Hot, moist forest districts are indeed those most favourable to the development of melanism among leopards, Travancore and the south of India generally being the regions on the west of the Bay of Bengal where these 'sports' are most common, while to the east they are still more abundant in Lower Burma and the Malay countries. In a paper contributed to the *Zoologist* for 1898 Colonel F.T. Pollok suggests that the reason for the prevalence of melanism in the latter district is that the leopards there habitually prey on gibbon apes, and that their sombre coloration renders them more inconspicuous than if they were spotted. He even goes so far as to say that under such conditions a leopard of the ordinary colour would starve. But this implies that all Malay leopards are black, which is certainly not the case; and it is also more than doubtful whether, in the case of an animal creeping along the arm of a tree, a uniformly black colour would not be more conspicuous than the ordinary spotted coat of the leopard. A white (albino) leopard has been recorded by Buchanan Hamilton.

The most essential difference between the habits of the leopard and the tiger is the facility with which the former animal can ascend trees; indeed, in some of the forest districts where its prey consists largely of monkeys, it may become an almost completely arboreal creature. This arboreal habit renders the leopard a more cunning animal than a tiger, since, when approaching a 'kill', it is stated to invariably scan the boughs above, whereas a tiger only does this when it has learnt caution from having been fired at from above on a previous occasion. It has been already mentioned that whereas a tiger always commences its meal by tearing at the hind-quarters of its victim, a leopard begins operations on the fore-quarters and viscera.

Leopards are on the prowl for prey throughout the night, dogs being their favourite victims in the neighbourhood of human habitations, while, as already said, in many forest districts they subsist chiefly on monkeys of various kinds. When a leopard takes to man-eating, it is even more to be dreaded than a tiger with similar propensities, since it will frequently not hesitate to burst through the frail walls of native huts and seize the inhabitants as they lie asleep. Colonel Pollok tells us that in certain portions of the Nizam's dominions the average deaths from man-eating leopards reached one *per diem*, while in others they were as many as two daily ! Even shikaris posted on platforms (*machans*) in trees have been carried off by the stealthy approach from behind of the very animals for which they were lying in wait.

In many parts of India the favourite haunts of leopards are rocky, scrub-clad hills, containing numerous clefts and caverns, in which they make their lairs. Water is much less essential to their well-being than is the case with the tiger, and they are not unfrequently found in completely dry districts in India, while in Somaliland they commonly dwell in such situations. In India, at any rate, these animals are generally found in pairs, and the cubs are born during February or March, the number in a litter being usually from two to four, although Colonel Pollok states that he has heard of as many as seven. It is a curious fact in connection with leopard cubs that the spotting is much less distinct than in the adult, the general colour being brownish. This is precisely the reverse of what occurs in the lion. As a rule, the leopard is a silent animal, although when charging it utters a short growl. Those best conversant with its habits in a state of nature state, however, that when on the prowl it occasionally gives vent to a harsh cry, quite different to the roar of a tiger, and somewhat intermediate between a grunt and a cough.

Although leopards were at one time hunted by the troopers of the Central Indian Horse by beating them out from patches of sugar-cane during the rainy season with the aid of a pack of dogs and then spearing them, while they are often speared by parties of two or three mounted Europeans, the more general plan is either to watch for them by night in a *machan* over a tethered bait or a 'kill', or to drive them from covert with a line of beaters. Machan-shooting is weary work, and requires a large stock of patience on the part of the lonely watcher. As leopards usually go in search of water between seven and eight in the evening, and again between five and six in

the morning, it is at such times that they most frequently approach
the bait, the majority of tethered baits being seized between the
time of sunset and an hour after. In the dim twilight the spots of
the leopard harmonise so exactly with the speckled shade of the
surrounding foliage that, unless the watcher makes the best use of
his eyes, the marauder will be only too likely to have sprung upon
the bait before its presence is even suspected.

The following hints on machan-shooting are given by an
anonymous writer in The Asian newspaper of 27 February 1900—

'If you have had a kill, go early to your machan, and take the
precaution to have the kill securely tied or hung to some fixed object,
or you may find the panther carry it off without giving you a chance.

'If you are to sit over a live goat, see first that the machan is so
constructed as to give you the advantage of rising ground if there
be any. Take care that the rope of the goat is not too long, or you
will find it perhaps difficult to get a shot from your circumscribed
look-out hole. If there is a little moonlight expected after dusk, try
and arrange your machan so as to have the light falling from behind
you on to the goat. Recollect the shadow cast by the moon. It is not
always easy to distinguish the shadow from the substance of the
goat, and the same is of course true of the panther. Take your time
in aiming, and if the panther is inextricably mixed up with the goat,
wait. Eventually the panther will conquer the goat and give you a
steady shot while sucking the blood from the neck.

'Don't fancy the panther will not come, once you have made
up your mind to sit up. Some are exceedingly crafty and suspicious,
and do not fail to observe the goat most carefully. Often the goat
ceases bleating simply from an access of fear; it has seen, heard, or
scented the panther. You will often see it, after standing or lying
carelessly, suddenly assume a rigid position, gradually moving its
head round, and sometimes by the action of its legs unmistakably

indicating that the foe is about. The goat will sometimes stamp on the ground and emit little snorts. Of course occasionally this may only indicate a hyaena, or a pig, or the insignificant mongoose, or a hare, but never neglect such indications.

'As to using slugs, I think you will do well to have a smooth-bore loaded with buck-shot. But stick to your rifle to the last possible moment. Slugs do not always penetrate between the ribs and reach a vital part, and they seldom leave a bloody trail. I have rarely found my 500 Express fail even when it was impossible to see the sights.'

The Sal Forests

CAPTAIN JAMES FORSYTH

Above Mandla, the valley of the Narbada opens out into a wide upland country, the main river, between this and Jubbulpor, joined by few and unimportant tributaries, here radiating like the fingers of a hand, and draining the rainfall of an extensive triangular plateau, known as the Mandla district. These converging valleys rise in elevation towards the south, where they terminate in a transverse range of hills, which sends down spurs between them, subdividing the drainage. The valleys themselves also successively rise in general elevation, by a step-like formation from west to east. Furthest to the west, that of the Banjar river possesses a general height of about 2,000 feet; next is that drained by the Ilalon and the Phen at about 2,300; still further to the east the basin of the Khormer has risen to about 2,800 feet; and furthest east of all is the plateau of Amarkantak, the chief source of the Narbada, which attains a general altitude

Excerpts of the essay 'The Sal Forests' taken from: Forsyth, Captain James. *The Highlands of Central India: Notes on Their Forests and Wild Tribes, Natural History and Sport* (London: Chapman and Hall Limited, 1889), pp. 369–401.

of about 3,300 feet, with smaller flat-topped elevations reaching to 4,000 feet above the sea. The hilly range which runs along the southern border of the district is called the Mykat, and overlooks, in a steep descent to the southward, a flat low-lying country called Chattisgarh, or 'the land of thirty-six forts'.

The elevated cradle of the infant Narbada, thus described, contains within its outer circle of hills an area of not less than 7,000 square miles; much of it, of course, of a broken and unculturable character, but comprising also in the valleys much of what may properly be called virgin soil of the finest quality. The Mykat range, and the radiating spurs which separate the plateau, are mostly clothed with forests of the sal tree, which, here as elsewhere, almost monopolises the parts where it grows. The saj alone grows in any quantity along with it. Some of the hills are covered with the ordinary species of forest trees of other parts; the species of vegetation appearing, as I have said before, to depend much on the geological formation.

The valleys themselves are generally open and free from all underwood, dotted here and there by belts and islands of the noble sal tree, and altogether possessing much of the character ascribed to the American prairies. In their lowest parts the soil is deep, black and rich, covered with a growth of strong tall grasses. As the valleys merge into the hilly ranges, the soils become lighter and redder, from the lateritie topping that here overlies the basaltic and granitic bases of the hills; the grasses are less rank and coarse; and in many places springs of clear cold water bubble up, clothing the country with belts of perpetual verdure, and conferring on it an aspect of freshness very remarkable in a country of such comparatively small elevation in the centre of India. Everything combines to deprive this region of the sterile and inhospitable appearance worn by even most upland tracts during the hot season. The sal tree is almost the only evergreen forest tree in India. Throughout the summer its glossy dark-green foliage reflects the light in a thousand vivid tints; and just when all other vegetation is at its worst, a few weeks before the gates of heaven are opened in the annual monsoon, the sal selects its opportunity of bursting into a fresh garment of the brightest and softest green. The traveller who has lingered till that late period in these wilds is charmed by the approach of a second spring, and it requires no slight effort to believe himself still in a tropical country. The atmosphere has been kept humid by the moisture from the broad sheets of water retained by the upland streams, which descends nightly in dews on the open valleys. The old grasses of the prairie have been burnt in the annual conflagrations, and a covering of young verdure has taken their place. Now and then the familiar note of the cuckoo* (identical with the European bird), and the voices of many birds, including the deep musical coo of the grand imperial pigeon, heighten the delusion. But for the bamboo thickets on the higher hills, whose light feathery foliage beautifully supplements the heavier masses of the sal that cling to their skirts, the scene would present nothing peculiar to the landscape of a tropical country.

The climate of these uplands is very temperate for this part of India, showing a mean of about 77 degrees of the thermometer during the hot season. The variation between the temperature of day and night is, however, considerable, ranging from about 50 degrees to 100 degrees as extremes during the hot season under canvas. It would of course be much more equable in a house, and the range is also far less on the higher plateaux than in the lower valleys. In the cold season (which corresponds to our winter) it generally descends at night to freezing-point in the open air, rising in a tent no higher than 65 degrees or 70 degrees in the middle of the day.

The country can scarcely be said to be populated at all, except within a short distance of Mandla itself, where the rich soil has been

---

* Cuculus canorus.

cultivated by an outlying colony of Hindus from the Lower Narbada valley. Mandla was at one time the seat of one of the Gond-Rajput ruling dynasties, and the remains of their forts and other buildings still crown in crumbling decay the top of many a forest-covered mound.

The Gonds are here a very poor and subdued race, long since weaned from their wild notions of freedom, with its attendant hardships and seclusion; but still unreached by the influence of the general advancement which has in some measure redeemed them in most parts from their state of practical serfdom to the superior races. They usually plough with cattle, instead of depending on the axe, and are nearly all hopelessly in debt to the money-lenders, who speculate in the produce they raise. There is no local market, and the difficulty of exporting grain over the seventy or eighty miles of atrocious road to the open country is such that the prices obtained for their produce are contemptible. They congregate in filthy little villages, overrun by poultry and pigs, and innocent of all attempt at conservancy.

Far superior to them in every respect are the still utterly unreclaimed forest Bygas, another aboriginal race, whose habitat is in the hills of the Mykat range and its spurs, which intersect these valleys. The same tribe extends over a vast range of forest-covered country to the west of Mandla, where we shall subsequently meet them again under the name of Bhumias. A few have somewhat modified their original habits, and live, along with the Gonds, in villages lower down the valleys. These have been slightly tainted with Hinduism, shave their elfin locks, and call themselves by a name denoting caste. But the real Byga of the hill ranges is still almost in a state of nature. They are very black, with an upright, slim, though exceedingly wiry frame, and showing less of the negretto type of feature than any other of these wild races. Destitute of all clothing but a small strip of cloth, or at most, when in full dress, with the addition of a coarse cotton sheet worn crosswise over the chest, with long, tangled, coal-black hair, and furnished with bow and arrow and a keen little axe hitched over the shoulder, the Byga is the very model of a hill aborigine. He scorns all tillage but the dhya clearing on the mountain-side, pitching his neat habitation of bamboo wicker-work, like an eagle's eyrie, on some hill-top or ledge of rock, far above the valleys penetrated by pathways; and ekes out the fruits of the earth by an unwearying pursuit of game. Full of courage, and accustomed to depend on each other, they hesitate not to attack every animal of the forest, including the tiger himself. They possess a most deadly poison wherewith they tip their little arrows of reed; and the most ponderous beast seldom goes more than a mile, after being pierced with one of these, without falling. The poison is not an indigenous one, but is brought and sold to them by the traders who penetrate these wilds to traffic in forest produce. I believe it to be an extract of the root of *Aconitum ferox*, which is used for a similar purpose by some of the tribes of the eastern Himalaya. The flesh is discoloured and spoilt for some distance round the wound. This is cut out, and the rest of the carcase is held to be wholesome food. Their bows are made entirely of the bamboo, 'string' and all; they are very neat, and possess wonderful power for their size. A good shot among them will strike the crown of a hat at fifty yards. Their arrows are of two sorts; those for ordinary use being tipped with a plain iron head, and feathered from the wing of the peafowl, while those intended for poisoning and deadly work have a loose head, round which the poison is wrapped, and which remains in the wound. These poisoned arrows are altogether remarkably similar to those used by the Bushmen of South Africa. Their axes are also of two sorts—one, like the ordinary axes of the Gonds, for cutting wood, and the other, a much more formidable implement, called a *tongia*, with a long semicircular blade like an ancient battle-axe in miniature. All the iron for these weapons, and for their agricultural instruments, is forged from the native ore of the hills, by a class called Agurias, who seem to be a section of the Gonds. A Byga has been known to attack and destroy a tiger with no other weapon than his axe. This little weapon is also used as a projectile, and the Byga will thus knock over hares, peafowl, etc., with astonishing skill.

Though thus secluded in the wilderness, the Mandla Byga is by no means extremely shy, and will placidly go on cutting his dhya while a train of strangers is passing him, when a wild Gond or Korku would have abandoned all and fled to the forest. They are truthful and honest almost to a fault, being terribly cheated in consequence in their dealings with the traders; and they possess the patriarchal form of selfgovernment still so perfectly, that nearly all their disputes are settled by the elders without appeal, though these, of course, under our alien system, possess no legal authority. Serious crime among them is almost unheard of. The strangest thing about them is that, though otherwise certainly the wildest of all these races, they have no aboriginal language of their own, speaking a rude dialect of which almost every word can be traced to the Hindi. They can also communicate with the Gonds in their language, though they do not use it among themselves. A similar case is that of the Bheels, in the western continuation of these hills, who, though also extremely wild, have no peculiar language of their own, and never have had, so far as history informs us. There are many points of resemblance between the Bygas and the Bheels, and there seems to be no evidence to connect either with the Kolarian or the Dravidian families of aborigines. Further inquiry may show them to be remnants of a race anterior in point of time to both, and from which the Hindi may have borrowed its numerous non-Sanscrit vocables. We know that, at an early period in Hindu history, Bheels held the country up to the river Jammi, which they do not now approach within many hundred miles.

There is every reason to believe that these Bygas are, if not autochthonous, at least the predecessors of the Gonds in this part of the hills. They consider themselves, and are allowed to be, superior to the Gonds, who may not eat with them, and who take their priests of the mysteries, or medicine-men, from among them. Theirs it is to hold converse with the world of spirits, who are everywhere present to aboriginal superstition; theirs it is to cast omens, to compel the rain, to charm away the tiger or disease. The Byga medicine-man fully looks his character. He is tall, thin, and cadaverous, abstraction and mystery residing in his hollow eyes. When wanted, he has to be sent for to some distant haunt of gnomes and spirits, and comes with charms and simples slung in the hollow of a bottle-gourd. A great necklace, fashioned with much carving from the kernels of forest fruits, marks his holy calling.

The Byga charmer's most dangerous duty is that of laying the spirit of a man who has been killed by a tiger. Man-eaters have always been numerous in Mandla, the presence during a part of every year of large herds of cattle fostering the breed, while their withdrawal at other times to regions where the timers cannot follow causes temporary scarcity of food, too easily relieved in the abundant tall grass cover by recourse to the killing of man; the desultory habits of the wild people, and the numbers of travellers who take this short route between the Narbada valley and the plains of Chattisgarh, furnishing them with abundant and easy victims. The Byga has to proceed to the spot where the death occurred—which is probably still frequented by the tiger—with various articles, such as fowls and rice, which are offered to the manes. A pantomime of the tragedy is then enacted by the Byga, who assumes the attitude of a tiger, springs on his prey, and devours a mouthful of the blood-stained earth. Eight days are allowed to pass; and should the Byga not, in the interval, be himself carried off by the tiger, the spirit is held to be effectually laid, and the people again resort to the jungle. The theory rests on the superstition, prevalent throughout these hills, that the ghost of the victim, unless charmed to rest, rides on the head of the tiger, and incites him to further deeds of blood, rendering him also secure from harm by his preternatural watchfulness. To remove pestilence or sickness, they have a pleasant notion that it must be transferred to someone else; and so they sweep their villages, after the usual sacrifices, and cast the filth on the highway or into the bounds of some other village.

The real Byga medicine-man possesses the gift of throwing himself into a trance, during which the afflatus of the Deity is supposed to be vouchsafed to him, communicating the secrets of the future. 1 never saw the performance myself, but persons who have affirm that it is too severe in its physical symptoms to be mere acting; and there is sufficient evidence from other quarters to prove that some persons can educate themselves into the power of passing into such fits at will, to lead us to credit the Byga at least with nothing worse than selfdeception in the matter, in religion the Bygas have admitted a few of the Hindu deities of the destructive type; but their chief reverence is paid to the spirits of the waste, and to Mother Earth, who is their tribal god. One of their tribal names is Bhumia, meaning 'people of the soil', and it is curious that among every aboriginal tribe of these hills, including the Bheels, the priests or medicine-men are called by the same name. The rite of charming the souls of deceased persons into some material object, before described, and which seems peculiar to these hills, is practised also by these Bygas.

A male Byga is easily distinguished from a Gond; but their women are scarcely in any respect different— perhaps a little blacker, but dressing in a similar manner, wearing the same ornaments (including a chignon of goat's hair), and, like them, also tattooed as to the legs. Though the Bygas are, like the Bheels, less given to congregate together in large villages than some other tribes, often indeed living in entirely detached dwellings, there are a good many villages of a considerable number of houses. These are arranged with much neatness in the form of a square, and the whole place is kept very clean.

The Byga is the most terrible enemy to the forests we have anywhere in these hills. Thousands of square miles of sal forest have been clean destroyed by them in the progress of their dhya cultivation, the ground being afterwards occupied by a dense scrub of low sal bushes springing from the stumps. In addition to this, the largest trees have everywhere been girdled by them to allow the gum resin of the sal (the dammer of commerce) to exude.

The dammer resin, called here dhok, is extensively used as a pitch in dockyards, and for coating commercial packages. It is extracted by cutting a ring of bark out of the tree three or four feet from the ground, when the gum exudes in large bubbles. Several half-circles are, however, equally effective, and do not destroy the life of the tree, like the former method. The ringing of sal trees has now been entirely prohibited within our territories; but I do not think that any more economical method has as yet been substituted, the vast area of sal in native states being sufficient to supply the present wants of the trade. The dammer is collected, and, together with lac dye, is exchanged for salt, beads, and arrow-poison, brought by peripatetic traders with pack-bullocks, who annually visit their wilds for the purpose. This may be said to be the only commercial transaction of the Byga in the whole year. He rarely visits the low-country markets, like the other tribes, and has scarcely a knowledge of coined money.

Fortunately the sal tree, unlike the teak, is possessed of a most inextinguishable reproductive power, the seeds being shed by every mature tree in millions, and ready to germinate at once in a favourable position. The seedlings shoot rapidly above the danger of jungle-fires, and grow straight and tall before branching out. The timber of the sal, if inferior to the teak for some purposes, such as carpentry and transverse beams, is superior for others, such as wheel-work and uprights, its straight, firm grain giving it immense power of resistance to crushing. It is almost the only timber tree of Upper India, where teak is unknown. The unlimited water-power of these rivers will supply the means of converting it on the spot; and the Narbada will form a highway for floating it to the open valley. Sal will not swim by itself, until seasoned for several years; but the hills produce an unlimited quantity of the finest bamboos, a bundle of which tied round a log will support it, and which are themselves of the highest economic value. At present these forests have scarcely been drawn on for the supply of timber, being distant from the Narbada some thirty or forty miles, without a road capable of conveying heavy timber. I have already remarked on the appearance of the sal tree. Singly it is a little formal in outline, though possessing a fine, firm aspect from its horizontal branching, bright evergreen leaves like broad lance-heads, and straight, tapering stem covered with grey and deeply-fissured bark. Its great charm, however, resides in the fresh, cool aspect of the masses and belts in which it chiefly grows.

Besides the dammer resin of the sal, several other kinds of minor forest produce are collected here, as in other tracts, for sale to the traders of the plains. Some of these have already been mentioned. Another is the stick-lac of commerce, which is deposited by an insect on the smaller twigs of several species of trees, among which *Butea frondosa*, *Schleichera trijuga* and *Zizyphus jujuba* are the principal. The twigs are broken off, and sold as they stand, looking like pieces of very dark red coral. About twenty pounds will be procured annually from a tree, so long as any of the insects are left on it to breed. But just as often as not the improvident wild man will cut down the whole tree to save himself the trouble of climbing. The inborn destructiveness of these jungle people to trees is certainty very extraordinary; even where it is clearly against their own interest, they cannot apparently refrain from doing wanton injury. A Gond or Byga passing along a pathway will almost certainly, and apparently unconsciously, drop his axe from the shoulder on any young sapling that may be growing by its side, and almost everywhere young trees so situated will be found cut half through in this manner. The stick-lac is manufactured into dye in considerable quantities at a factory in Jubbulpur, whose agents penetrate the remotest corners of these jungles in search of the raw material.

The cocoons of the wild tusser silk-moth are also collected in great numbers for sale to the caste of silk-spinners who live by this business in the villages of the plains. Experience has shown that these moths will not breed a second generation of healthy silk-producing insects in captivity, and a fresh supply is therefore procured annually from their native hills. They live chiefly on the leaves of the saj tree, whose foliage, being deciduous, would not afford safety to the insect in its chrysalis stage, if the cocoon were attached, as other species are, to the leaf alone. The instinct of the little creature teaches it therefore to anchor its cocoon by a strong silken rope to the leaf-stalk, where it sways about in safety after every leaf has dropped from the tree. The cocoons brought from the jungles by the breeders are attached to pollarded saj trees, grown near their villages, till the moths have hatched and paired, when the females are captured and made to lay their eggs in close vessels, where they are incubated by heat. The worms reared from the eggs are again placed on the saj trees, where they form their cocoons, which are then spun into the rough silk known as 'tusser'. The business is a very precarious one, much depending for success on favourable weather. Superstition of course seizes this uncertainty for her own, and the purchased blessings of the Byga priest must accompany the cocoons from their native hills, if the breeder of the plains is to expect success.

Besides such scanty exportation of the minor produce of these wilds as I have described, almost their only economic use has hitherto been the splendid grazing they afford for countless herds of cattle, annually brought to them from great distances in the open country on both sides during the hot season. Fine grass and abundance of shade and water make this one of the finest grazing countries in all India, and the amount of wealth which thus actually seems to depend on its continuance as a waste is very great.

At first sight some hesitation might be felt at the prospect of these great grazing-grounds being reclaimed for cultivation, when it is considered how all-essential to the life of a country like India is the breeding of large stocks of oxen. Here the draught ox takes the place of the farm-horse and the steam-engine of England. Cattle are bred, not as an article of food, but as affording perhaps the only description of power by which the operations of agriculture could be performed at all. Horses could not take their place in converting the hard, burnt-up soils, under the blazing sun of the season, when ploughing and sowing the autumn crop goes on, nor, so far as we know the resources of the land, could steam power, even if otherwise suitable, find sufficient fuel at anything like a moderate cost. Thus it may not have been without a teaching of far-seeing policy that the Hindi has been prohibited by his religion from converting the race of horned cattle to the purposes of food. It may be true that the rigid prohibition against touching the carcases of such animals, or in any way trafficking in their death, may have excluded the Hindu cattle-owner from much legitimate profit in the way of leather, horn, tallow, glue, etc.; but it is impossible to draw fine shades of distinction in religious sanctions, and if, as is probable, the slaughter of cattle useful for the plough could not be otherwise prevented, then the sanctification of the animal from all such uses was probably a measure of the highest policy. Even looked on as an article of food, it is probable that the sacredness of the cow has been productive of more gain than loss, milk and butter being much more wholesome articles of diet than beef in a hot climate. Certainly, any measure which would be likely to endanger the existing supply of plough-cattle would be highly objectionable. But I think that no apprehension of the sort need be entertained from the probable reclamation of such tracts as the Mandla savannahs. Sufficient forest land must always remain in the higher regions to furnish the green bite at the end of the hot season, which is all that is necessary to tide the herds over the most trying part of the year, and, for the rest, the people will soon learn to do as other countries have done, and as other parts of India even have done, namely, devote a part of the cultivated area to the raising of green pasture, by irrigation, for the cattle. This fine natural pasture is no doubt a great advantage; but it is not at all indispensable even in India.

The resources of the country in iron and other mineral wealth have never been fully examined, though it is evident on the surface that they are abundant. Gold is washed out of the sands of more than one of the streams, in small quantities, however, which barely repay the labour, and it is probable that its lodes are buried in the quartz of the primitive rocks deep below the flow of volcanic material that has overlaid them.

In the matter of climate, like all uncleared regions in this latitude at so low an elevation, the tract is subject to malarious fever during the months of October to January. But experience shows that this influence lasts only so long as the country continues uncleared.

It is probable that the Lower Narbada valley was equally unhealthy at one time, yet it is now as healthy as any part of the country. Several stations in these provinces have been set down in the middle of jungles with as evil a reputation as this, and along with the clearance of the jungle the fever was found to disappear. The Wynaad, Assam, and Cachar are also standing instances of the successful occupation of malarious countries by the help of European enterprise. The malaria excepted, the climate is highly favourable to colonisation, considering the situation of the tract. No region out of the great mountain ranges could probably be pointed to as possessing such advantages of coolness and freshness as are here conferred by the elevated situation, abundance of moisture, and its attendant evergreen verdure.

As for the obstacles supposed to be presented by the rank vegetation and noxious animals, they are chiefly imaginary. Immense plains lie ready for the plough, if merely the coarse natural grasses were cleared away, there being no brushwood or heavy timber to speak of. The luxuriance of these grasses is only evidence of the fatness of the land that lies below; and a torch applied in the month of May will, over large tracts, remove all obstacle to the immediate application of the plough. The wild animals, here as elsewhere, would retire before the axe and plough of the settler. Such as are noxious to human life are not really more so here than in many other much more open parts of the country. In the districts of Dom and Betul there is certainly a larger number of tigers in the same area than in Mandla, and there they have not been found to constitute any serious obstacle to the steady advancement of population and tillage.

I am not one of those who believe that Europeans can ever labour profitably with their own hands in the 'plains' of India; and even at this elevation I believe that the power of the sun, although much alleviated by the coolness of the breezes, the low temperature of the nights, and the freshness of the vegetation, would still be prohibitive of severe manual labour by natives of a temperate region. But I think that we have here a tract eminently fitted to yield results from the application of European energy, intelligence, and capital to the supervision and direction of native labour.

The great difficulty would be to obtain the labour to supervise. I doubt if the regular Hindu cultivators of the plains outside could be induced to move into these wilds by any temptation, so long as they can obtain a pittance where they are. The aborigines are too timid and unstable to furnish reliable workmen. I would rather look to the teeming millions of the coast districts to furnish the needful supply of labourers, if these inland wastes are to be reclaimed with any reasonable period of time. It really seems to be matter for astonishment that these littoral races have for many years shown themselves to be ready to cross the seas to the West Indies, Mauritius, and other distant countries, and have actually been transported thither in great numbers, while all the time vast areas of the finest land are pining for labour in the interior of their own country. There cannot be a doubt which they would most willingly go to, in order to escape from their densely crowded condition at home, were the inducements offered to them the same. What has tempted them to other countries has been the superior wages which their industries could afford to offer; and in India, wherever, as in Assam, Cachar, and the Wynaad, such articles of European demand as coffee, tea, etc., have attracted European enterprise, and where similar wages have been held out, an abundant supply of labour has been furnished by these fountains of population. What appears to be necessary, then, to effect the rapid reclamation of these wilds, is the introduction of some special industry which will attract the European energy and capital which alone can ever effect the movement of Indian labour in large bodies from one part of the country to another. That there are such industries capable of introduction there cannot be a doubt.

At present cattle-breeding would seem to be the most promising opening, both because it wants the fewest hands, and because the absence of roads is of less consequence in such a business.

Before leaving the subject of these waste lands, I should refer to the only attempt ever made to form a settlement in them under European supervision, and which ended in lamentable failure. Some thirty years ago four German missionaries attempted to form a colony among the aboriginal tribes, on the Moravian system, in one of these upland valleys. They selected a spot just under the Amarkantak plateau, near a small village called Karinjca, in the middle of a fine plain of rich soil, a few miles south of the Narbada. The place had an elevation of about 2,700 feet, and was well situated in every respect but one. In a country abounding with shade and water, they pitched on a bare mound without an evergreen tree, and more than two miles distant from the nearest running water. They went out in the hot weather, and failed to prepare sufficient shelter before the arrival of the rainy season. Thus they remained exposed to constant damp and cold winds, and dependent for their water on a small stagnant pool polluted by the drainage of decaying vegetation. The result was death from cholera, or some other malignant bowel complaint, of three out of the four, and the retreat of the only survivor. However worthy of praise, such an enterprise cannot be looked on as a fair experiment. But it cast a gloom over the prospect of further attempts of the same sort, and has never again been repeated. The example of the missions to the Kols of Bengal and the Karens of Burma, where the combination of profitable industrial enterprise with theological teaching has been found to be singularly effective in the propagation of the Gospel among aboriginal races, may point to the desirability of some such system being attempted among the unsophisticated savages of these wilds by those who are now preaching in vain to the semi-Hindu tribes further west.

Some time ago a French gentleman took up a considerable tract of the finest land in one of these valleys. But it soon appeared that he had no intention of real colonisation, and had, in fact, been merely speculating on the value of the forest produce of the land. This and other symptoms of land-jobbing have, I believe, induced some reconsideration of the rules for the sale of the fee simple of waste lands. One thing may be relied on, however—that whatever title a settler may here obtain from the Government will be an absolute one, every existing or possible private interest having been fully determined before the available wastes were declared by law to be state property.

In such a well-watered, shady, and grassy region as this Upper Narbada valley, it is inevitable that wild animals should abound.

The hilly ranges which separate the valleys contain the bison, the sambar, and the black bear, like similar tracts in other parts of the province. These are animals peculiar to no part of India, and the same may be said of the spotted deer, which affects the densely wooded banks of the larger streams. But, as I have said, we are here within the limits of the great sal belt, and come upon some animals which I have noticed as coinciding in range therewith.

Chief in interest among these is the beautiful twelve-tined deer (*Rueervus duvaucellii*), called by some the Bara-singha, a name which simply means 'twelve- tined', and which is applied also to the Kashmir stag (*C. Cashmiriensis*). In size it is intermediate between the sambar and the spotted deer, and almost the same as the red deer of Scotland. In colour it is a reddish brown during the cold season, passing through a bright rufous chestnut in spring to a rich golden red in summer. The antlers are very handsome, and differently shaped from those of any other deer in the world. They have but one basal tine over the forehead, no median tines at all, and all the other branches arranged at the summit of the beam. Here they show a tendency to approach the Rusine type, to which belong the sambar and the axis, the beam being first divided into a terminal fork, each branch of which afterwards splits into several points. Usually the outward or anterior branch bears three such points, and the inward or posterior two, making, with the brow-antler, six points on each horn. Very old stags sometimes have more; but, as in the *Rusine*, when there are more than three the extra ones are abnormal monstrosities, and the antlers are usually unsymmetrical and stunted in size. The horns are grayish in colour, and of a smoother surface than those of the sambar. They are not nearly so massive, nor so long, but have a very handsome outward sweep, which renders them, I think, more effective as a trophy for the deerstalker. They are very difficult to procure fully developed and perfect. They are cast more regularly,

I think, than those of the *Rusince*; and as the stags seem to be very combative, some of the points are usually broken off soon after they lose the velvet at the close of the rainy season, when their haunts first become accessible to the sportsman. In form the Rucervus is one of the most beautiful of the family—lightly and gracefully made, and with a stately carriage; and altogether, with his splendid golden colour and finely-shaped antlers, this stag is not surpassed, I think, in appearance, by any member of the deer tribe.

This animal has been called in north-east India the 'swamp deer', but here he is not observed to be particularly partial to swampy ground. They graze in the mornings and evenings, chiefly along the smaller streams, and by springs, where the grass is green, in the open valleys, and rest during the day about the skirts of the sal forest. A favourite midday resort is in the shade of the clumps of sal dotted about the open plain, at some distance from the heavy forest. They are not nearly so nocturnal in habits as the sambar, being often found out grazing late in the forenoon, and again early in the afternoon; and I do not think they wander about all night like the sambar. Their midday rest is usually of a few hours only, but during that time they conceal themselves in the grass much after the manner of the sambar. I have never heard of their visiting cultivated tracts, like the latter; nor can I learn that their apparent adherence to the sal forest is due to their employing any part of that tree as food.

In the middle of the day the red deer (so they are called by natives, and often by Europeans) may be shot by beating the grass with elephants in the manner before described. During the height of the cold weather many parts of this tract can hardly be traversed except on an elephant; and in such places shooting would otherwise be impossible, owing to the height and thickness of the grass jungle. In the course of a day's beating of this sort in the Mandla district a very great variety of game may easily be met with. On one occasion, when spending Christmas with two friends in the lovely Matiari valley, a day's march east of the station of Mandla, we secured, I think, a specimen of nearly every kind of game to be found in the country, excepting the bison and the panther. On the 26th we marched from a place called Bartola to Gobri, both on the Matiari—a clear sparkling stream that here runs through a valley, filled with long grass cover, and bounded on either side by chains of low hills, flat on the tops, and clothed with low tree jungle and bamboos on their sides. We took separate lines, F. going by the pathway, D. along the tops of the hills on one side, while I beat along the river below on an elephant. I had not gone far before I put up a large herd of sambar in long grass, and, firing right and left, dropped one small stag, and heavily wounded a very large fellow with splendid antlers and as black as a buffalo. I got off, and tracked the wounded animal for about three miles by his blood, through the long, dewy grass, till I was as thoroughly wetted through as if I had been wading in a tank, when, as the deer had reached heavy bamboo cover, and seemed to be still strong, I gave it up, and again made for the river. On the way I came on a herd of red deer, grazing about in an opening in the low jungle, where a fine spring kept the grass beautifully green. They saw me before I was within shot, however, and retreated into grass cover. Waiting a little, I got on the elephant, and proceeded to beat the long grass; and, after going about a quarter of a mile, started the herd, which must have contained fully thirty individuals. They dived into a deepish hollow, filled with low brushwood, in front of me, and I waited on the edge for their appearance on the far side. Presently they clattered up in single file, stags and does intermixed, the last of all being a very large dark red stag, with beautiful antlers that seemed almost to overpower him as he slowly trotted up the rise. I had the sight of the double rifle bearing full on his broad back, and was just touching the trigger when the man behind me seized and detained my arm in a vice-like grasp. The moment was lost, and I turned viciously on the culprit, who, however, pointed silently to an object in a tree close to our heads. It was a huge colony of bees—the terrible *Bonhra*, whose swarms had, a march or two before, routed our whole following, leaving a good-sized baggage pony dead upon the ground. Lucky it was I had not fired, and I thought little of the lost stag in the hurry to get out of so dangerous a vicinity. About half a mile further on, near the river, a spotted doe leaped out of a patch of grass, and scoured across the plain. It was too tempting, she looked so round and fat; and a snap shot rolled her over, shot through the loins. We were now not far from camp, and I was beating through some longish grass, when a full, round countenance was seen peering over the top of it at the advancing elephant. I did not make it out for a while, and presently it disappeared, the motion of the grass showing the progress of a large body towards the river. A little further on it stopped, and the round face again glared at me over the grass. Surely it must be a tiger? A glimpse of a striped red hide settled the question, and I moved a little down to cut her off from the river bed. All was motionless for a few minutes, and then again the slowly waving grass showed the stealthy progress towards the deep gully in which ran the river. A shallow ravine was a little ahead, down which she could steal unobserved, except in one place, where a little jungle pathway crossed it, and I took up a place commanding this at about sixty yards, waiting with cocked rifle and beating heart. Now she is close to the opening, the grass rustling gently above her. Now she sneaks rapidly across, crawling low, but halts for a moment to look again before entering the further cover. Fatal pause! A ball speeds through her shoulder, and, turning with a roar, she gallops back again up the hollow. I thought she meant a charge, and hastily reloaded the discharged barrel of my breechloader, as I had only one gun out, being on a pad. But she left the nala, when nearly opposite me, on the wrong side. I think she must have forgotten, for she evidently looked out for her assailant, jumping high above the grass at every bound—a really beautiful sight, with her very bright-coloured skin, hair erect, and tail streaming behind her. About the third bound I caught her with another bullet, and she fell, crumpled up in mid-air, for all the world just like a partridge struck full by a charge of shot. She was lying stone-dead when I came up, and no wonder, for the ball had entered near her tail, traversed the whole length of her body, and was resting under the skin of her forehead. The rifle was a twelve-bore breech-loader, on my own spherical ball principle, the penetration of which may be judged of by this performance. The first shot was a little high on the shoulder, but would soon have hilled her, and fully accounted for her confnsion of ideas. She had evidently been lying on the watch for spotted deer coming to drink. A large herd of them broke out of the grass while our interview was in progress. Coming to camp, I found that F. had shot a black buck antelope on the road; while D. returned with a young *bara-singha* stag and a spotted deer. In the evening F. went out, and killed a large bear, which came down to the river to drink beside him. Next day we were almost equally fortunate, though no tiger was met with; and we spent a Christmas of considerable joviality in that remote wilderness, the dinner consisting, as far as I recollect, of a (peacock) turkey and sambar tongue, supported by roast haunch of red-deer venison, as *pièces de résistance*, with cheetul cutlets and fillet of nilgai veal as *entrées*, followed up by boiled quails and roasted teal, and concluded by the orthodox plum-pudding and mince-pies out of Crosse and Blackwell's tins. Sundry glasses of whisky–toddy, imbibed round a rattling bonfire lit in front of the tents, were fully justified by the really severe cold after sunset. Stalking the *bara-singha*, however, affords the finest sport; and from the less exclusively nocturnal habits of the animal, as well as the open character of the country, resembles deerstalking in Scotland more than any other of our field sports.

When hurrying through this country in January, *en route* to the eastern forests, I halted for two days in the upper valley of the Halon to stalk the red deer, which I had never before seen. The grass was very thick and long, and, being still green, was entirely unburnt. At a place called Motinala, where a deep branching watercourse crosses the pathway several times, I was walking ahead of my followers, when I came on the remains of a poor wanderer, who had evidently not long before been killed by a tiger. He was a religious mendicant; and his long iron tongs, begging-bowl hollowed from a skull, and cocoa-nut hooka were scattered about in the bottom of the nala, where he had been resting on his weary march, together with tresses of his long matted hair and a shred or two of cloth. The bones were all broken to pieces, and many of them were missing altogether. A Banjara drover had been taken off near the same spot about a week before, so that it was not without some misgivings that I wandered off the road through the long grass to look for red deer towards the skirts of the hills. To hunt for the tiger in such an ocean of grass-cover would have been hopeless. I skirted the hills to the right of the road from here to the camping-ground at Mangli, very soon getting drenched to the skin passing through the high grass dripping with the morning dew. Towards the hills the grass was shorter, and the plain much cut up by deep fissures in the black, heavy soil. I saw several small herds of deer wending their way towards the clumps of sal forest on the skirt of the hills before I found any in a position that would admit of stalking. At last I marked a small parcel of hinds, with two fair-looking stags, disappear over a low rising ground, slowly feeding their way towards the forest; and making a long detour to gain the shelter of a deep crack, which led into the valley they had entered, I stalked almost into the middle of them before I was aware. My first intimation of the fact was the sharp bark of a hind, who had observed the top of my head over the bank, and the next moment a rush of feet informed me that the herd was off. Stepping on to the bank, I made a clean miss of the first running shot; but, taking more time with the second barrel, I saw the hindmost stag reel and almost fall over to the shot. He made off, however, along with the herd; but presently left them, and took a line of his own towards the long grass-cover in the middle of the plain. I soon hit on his track where he had entered the grass, and found a little blood; but as the grass was a long way over my head, I sent back for the elephant with which to beat him out. Following the blood-marks on the yellow stems for about a mile, we started him out of a patch of grass near the river, and I shot him through the back as he ran away.

The next day, being encamped at Topla, in the centre of a wide valley among the sal forest, I went out in the afternoon towards the Halon river. Here the country was open and prairie-like, short grass plains, dotted with clumps of sal, intervening between the heavier masses of forest. The river was very bright and clear, running over a pebbly bed. I took out two young half-bred hounds, between the Rampur breed and the Scotch deerhound, in the hope of getting them a run at a wounded red deer, as they were as yet guiltless of blood. Their mother, and the bull mastiff 'Tinker', of wolf renown, accompanied to help them in the kill. A couple of lithe blacks, and nearly naked Bygas, with their war-axes, guided the party. We wandered a good many miles in the early afternoon without coming on game, but I, at least, was gratified by the delightful park-like scenery. About four o'clock, by the advice of the Bygas, we sat down on a little eminence crowned by a clump of sal trees, to watch for deer coming out to drink or feed. Very soon a good-sized herd suddenly appeared in the middle of a long, flat stretch of grass-land beyond the river; and after stretching themselves, and enjoying a game at romps, commenced feeding pretty quickly down towards the bank of the river. We at once retreated over the bank of our knoll; and, getting into a hollow protected by a fringe of bushes, crept up to the banks and again reconnoitred. They were quite unsuspicious, the wind being highly favourable; and they seemed likely to come and drink in our very faces. When within a few hundred yards, however, they halted a long time behind a little rising ground. I was in agony lest the dogs should make us known, as they were dreadfully excited by the restraint of the stalks, and seemed to know perfectly well that there was something to hunt at hand. Presently a single hind topped the rise, and for full five minutes stood sniffing round in all directions, her great ears cocked in aid of her sense of smell. At last she seemed to be satisfied, and moved slowly forwards, now pausing to crop a mouthful of grass, and then again starting and looking about as if she had heard or smelt something. A stag now walked up past her, and without the least precaution came boldly on to the water, which he entered about a hundred yards above our post. The rest of the herd were still mostly hidden by the rise. Creeping through the bushes I prepared to fire at the stag, and gave orders for the hounds to be slipped at once after I should fire. I was barely in time to secure a shot, before the stag, alarmed by a yelp from one of the dogs, turned to flee up the bank. As it was I dropped him on the pebbly bank, shot through the shoulder; and, turning the rifle on the hind who was pausing startled at the shot, the other bullet passed through her thigh, injuring the hip joint. She fell on her hind quarters for a few moments, but presently recovered, and made off after the herd across the flat. The four dogs had sprung from the slips, and splashed through the shallow stream before she had well got on her legs; and they very nearly had her before she got fairly into her pace. Then, however, she distanced them at once for a few hundred yards, when the old bitch 'Bell', who was extremely fast, began to draw steadily up to her. The pups were a hundred yards behind, giving tongue like foxhounds, and old Tinker laboured along scarcely half-way from where they had started. Bell was very near the hind, when I saw her disappear bodily into a hole. But the deer was now failing fast; and, seeing no chance of making the forest, turned round and came back towards the river. The pups and Tinker now made up considerably by cutting off the corner, and very soon the brindled one, 'Sheroo', who was rather the faster, was racing alongside of her, making uncertain snatches at the shoulder. The yellow dog soon joined him, and together they managed to throw over the deer just as she reached the bank of the river. They all three rolled down the bank together; and before the deer could recover herself Tinker was up and pinned her by the throat. The bitch was not far behind, and among them they nearly tore the poor animal limb from limb. Fearing a row between Tinker and the young dogs I ran up as fast as possible; but a Byga with his axe was before me, and attempted to get the quarry from the dogs. He didn't know Tinker, however, who loosed his hold on the deer's throat only to fly at the Byga. The latter defended himself as well as he could with his axe-handle, very thoughtfully for such a savage, not attempting to use the head; but he had several pretty severe bites in the arms and legs before I could arrive to his rescue. As a rule Tinker was as quiet as a lamb with men; but when roused by blood he was a perfect devil; and as his size and weight were immense I was often rather afraid of him myself. Poor fellow, his formidable aspect and a few outbursts of this sort were the death of him, being poisoned by a dog boy a few months afterwards. Bell broke her neck by chasing an antelope down a blind well, a few marches after the hunt I have related; the best of the two pups was carried off by a leopard or hyaena; and altogether I was so disgusted with the bad luck I had always had in keeping large dogs in India that I gave it up altogether; and I cannot say that I found very much loss accrue to my sport in consequence. I believe they lose more wounded animals, by driving them out of reach, than they recover.

On the way back I shot another hind, who stood too long to gaze at the unwonted intruders, and saw the tracks of a wild elephant sinking deep into the soft, black soil. I was told afterwards that this elephant was one which had broken loose from captivity about ten

years previously, and had since inhabited the dense covers about the
head of the Halon river. He afterwards annoyed the forest officers
not a little by systematically demolishing all the masonry boundary
pillars erected by them round the reserved forest. Really wild
elephants do not come so far west as this; the country to the east of
Amarkantak (the source of the Narbada), or at the most the Samiri
valley, a little nearer than that place, being their most westerly range
in this part of India. Formerly, however, the whole of this country,
and far to the west of it, was the home of the wild elephant. The
etymology of many names, such as the 'elephant enclosure', the
'elephant pool', etc., would suffice to indicate this; but, besides,
we have it distinctly recorded, in that valuable work, the 'Institutes
of Akber', that in the sixteenth century elephants were found and
captured in the Narbada valley as far west as the Bijagarh and Handia
Sirkars,* which lie partly to the west of the meridian of the present
military stations of Mhow and Asirgarh. This is probably the most
westerly range of the wild elephant that has been recorded; and their
subsequent disappearance over so large a tract of country speaks
volumes for the advancement which has taken place in that period.

The night I was at Topla, two tigers roared loudly round about
the camp. We were pitched in a little glade in the sea of grass, and
the effect in the clear, cold night was very fine. The night voice
of the tiger has a very impressive sound, conveying, though not
nearly so loud as the bray of a jackass, the idea of immense power,
as it rolls and trembles along the earth. Four months later, when I
was encamped near Matin, in the forests of the far east, I listened
one night to the most remarkable serenade of tigers I ever heard. A
peculiar, long wail, like the drawn-out mew of a huge cat, first rose
from a river course a few hundred yards below my tent. Presently
from a mile or so higher up the river came a deep, tremendous

---

* Gladwin's *Ayeen Akbery*, vol. ii, p. 249.

roar, which had scarcely died away ere it was answered from behind the camp by another, pitched in a yet deeper tone, startling us from its suddenness and proximity. All three were repeated at short intervals, as the three tigers approached each other along the bottoms of the deep, dry watercourses, between and above which the camp had been pitched. As they drew together the noises ceased for about a quarter of an hour; and I was dozing off to sleep again, when suddenly arose the most fearful din near to where the tigress had first sounded the love-note to her rival lovers, a din like the caterwauling of midnight cats magnified a hundredfold. Intervals of silence, broken by outbursts of this infernal shrieking and moaning, disturbed our rest for the next hour, dying away gradually as the tigers retired along the bed of the river. In the morning I found all the incidents of a three-volume novel in feline life imprinted on the sand; and marks of blood showed how genuine the combat part of the performance had been. For the assurance of the timid, I may as well say that I have never had my camp actually invaded by a tiger, though constantly pitched, with a slender following, and without any sort of precaution, in the middle of their haunts. It strikes a stranger to jungle ways a little oddly, perhaps, to see a man in the warm summer nights calmly take his bed out a hundred yards from the tents, lie down under the canopy of heaven, listen, pipe in mouth, for half an hour to the noises of wild animals, and then placidly fall asleep. He soon learns to do the same himself.

About the end of the rains, in September and October, the red deer colleet in large herds on the tops of the plateaux; and I have been told of assemblages of several hundred heads at that season. They are then beginning to rut, and are very easy to get at, the Gonds and Bygas killing great numbers with their axes, aided by their strong, tall dogs. The best heads are to be got from these people... I myself never got a complete head with more than ten points, though I have secured some heavier than the twelve-pointed one... Its length is 33½ inches round the curve of each antler, and extreme spread 36 inches. There are few larger in the forests.

In the rains the wild buffalo wanders in herds all over these Mandla highlands. They mostly disappear, however, when the tame cattle are brought up to graze in the open season, a few only lingering in the most secluded valleys; and they must then be sought in the less accessible jungles to the south and west. Thither I must carry the reader to introduce him to the animal, as I never was in the Mandla district at the time when the buffaloes are found there.

The Bats

EDWARD HAMILTON AITKEN

'Eye of newt and toe of frog,
Wool of bat and tongue of dog,
Adder's fork and blind worm's sting,
Lizard's leg and owlet's wing.'

Witches seem to hang their caldron from the lamp-hook in the centre of the ceiling, and every now and then it boils over. The 'tongue of dog' is wanting this morning, and the wing is a sparrow's, not an owlet's, but the rest of the ingredients seem to be *as per recipe*. In these materialistic days it is taken for granted that the witch in question is a rat; but that at least is a delusion. No rat in the flesh could get to a hook situated in the very middle of a smooth ceiling unless it had wings, and we have been spared winged rats. I protest in all conscience they are bad enough with four legs and

Essay taken from: Aitken, Edward Hamilton. *The Tribes on My Frontier: An Indian Naturalist's Foreign Policy*, eighth edition (Calcutta and Simla: Thacker, Spink & Co., 1914), pp. 64–74.

a tail. No; few eyes have rested on the embodiment of hideousness from whose foul repast these crumbs have dropped. The demon bat does not go forth to do its deeds of darkness until the shades of night are falling, and as soon as

> 'The cock, that is the trumpet to the morn,
> Doth with his lofty and shrill-sounding throat
> Awake the god of day,'

it retires, like a guilty ghost, to its dark haunt among the rafters of some deserted godown. But in the small hours of the morning I have risen, when I heard its jaws at work,

> 'Feeding like horses when you hear them feed,'

and, quietly shutting the windows, have made it a prisoner, and in the morning there it was, hanging from the hook, its hyaena eyes glaring at me and a restless tremor playing over the thin membrane of its enormous ears. Very microphones those ears are, fit to catch the gentlest rustle of the feathers of a dreaming sparrow. Another pair of little trumpets of semi-transparent skin, like subordinate ears, rise from the nose, to gather the faintest odour of the sleeping prey as it floats past upon the air. To this extraordinary detective apparatus the demon bat adds a pair of ample wings of the softest vellum, on which it glides noiseless and ghostlike among the trees, or up and down the verandah, under the eaves of the roof. It scents a sparrow asleep, with its head cosily buried in its wing. The sparrow has a dream, a dreadful dream; it starts and raises its head and gives a piercing shriek, and the curtain falls. The sparrow is now hanging limp and lifeless from the jaws of the shadowy spectre, which flits in at the window and up to its favourite hook. In the morning two wings are lying beside the flower-vase upon the table, and perhaps a beak, for though the demon bat eats the head, skull and all, before any other part, it often leaves the beak. If the *hamal* is up before his *sahib* in the morning, he sweeps the remains away, and no one is a bit the wiser. That a sparrow's wings should occur on the table does not strike him as a phenomenon requiring explanation, especially if he found frogs' feet or a mouse's tail, or the remains of a little bat, on the same spot the morning before. The demon bat has a miniature, very much inferior to itself in size and ugliness, which I hold responsible for the grasshoppers' legs and wings of death's-head moths which I find about one particular corner of the dressing-room. I caught the transgressor once almost *flagrante delicto*, and sentenced it to be put under chloroform and examined. On recovering from the effects of the chloroform it was set free, for I abhor taking life needlessly. Jerdon puts this and the demon under different *genera*, and calls the one *Hipposideros* and the other *Megaderma*. It does not appear to me that they should be classed among bats at all. They seem rather to be a sort of incarnations of Satan, and might serve as models to Gustave Dore illustrating 'Paradise Lost'.

When we speak of the bat we generally have in mind a little animal which spends the day in crevices about the eaves, or in chinks of the window sunshades, squeaking and quarrelling on a small scale with its neighbour, and at dusk sallies forth after mosquitos. With its wrinkled face and small peering eyes it is a type of the race, a very estimable, inoffensive, and humdrum race. Beyond this in their praise it would be affectation to go: their virtues are not of the striking sort. One feels grateful to them, of course, for their unostentatious labours in keeping down mosquitos, small beetles, and flies, but Dr George Smith could not make a biography out of them. No animal abhors the honest light of day more cordially than the common bat. Even *Lucifuga blatta*, the cockroach, will creep out from its hiding-place under the table when it smells that the lid has been left off the butter-dish; and as for the owl, that bird of night, I never saw one yet, any hour of the twenty-four, which had not a very large round eye fixed on me. But a bat in daylight feels worse than

Hercules when he put on the coat with which his spouse presented him and suffered prickly heat. The prophet who says that the people will cast their idols to the moles and to the bats must have been a naturalist. Nature furnishes no more striking figure. Terminus and Priapus will lie neglected and half buried in the earth, obstructing the burrowing mole, while the Lares and Penates will be put away with other rubbish in some old lumber-room or garret, heavy with the smell of long-unmolested bats.

Catching bats with a butterfly-net and examining them is a good pastime for cold weather evenings. There are more kinds of them than I can tell the use of, small ones and smaller ones, largish ones with yellow breasts, pug-nosed ones and others with more prominent snouts, some thick and podgy, and one slim fellow with wings so long that they have to be folded a dozen times, more or less, before the animal can accommodate them about its person. This last is the one which you sometimes see shooting through the sky at express speed, chattering to itself in a shrill key. It is not to be caught with butterfly-nets or any such gins.

But after all, what have we to do with these. 'Of all the wild-fowl included under the name of bats, the only one that really comes into the foreground of Indian life is the fruit-bat or flying-fox. This animal has what I consider a handsome face, with large soft eyes, and would not be a bat at all but for two characteristic points, a strong batty smell and an insatiable craving for strife. Flying-foxes carry this last trait further than any others of the tribe. Considering that they spend the night filling their stomachs with indigestible green fruits, it is nothing strange that they should be dyspeptic and disagreeable by morning; the odd thing is that, in order to be within quarrelling distance of each other, they all must needs sleep on one tree, generally a huge tamarind with accommodation for two or three hundred. Before a dozen have gathered there is a misunderstanding between two which want the uppermost branch.

'That's my place.' 'I had it yesterday.' 'You hadn't.' 'I had.' 'You hadn't.' 'I had.' 'Hands off.' 'Whom arc you shoving?' Mutual recriminations follow, and from words they proceed to blows. One is dislodged and flies round to the other side of the treo, where it is greeted by a chorus of growls, 'No room here!' but it plumps into the middle of the objectors, and three lose their hold. Then the brawl becomes general and ends in a regular *fracas*. As the sun grows hot they cool down a little, but the fire is only smouldering, and may break out again at any time. These wranglings often lead indeed to the most scandalous scenes, as every one knows who has lived near a bats' roosting tree. Such trees are not so common about Bombay as they are up country, bccause every Goanese cook plots against the life of the flying-fox.

The bat is one of the unclean birds mentioned in the 11th chapter of Leviticus, which the Jews were forbidden to eat, but Pedro rejoices in his Christian liberty, and reckons it second only to roast pig. He hankers after even the small fruit-bat, that lesser edition of the flying-fox, which has such a *penchant* for the flowers of the plantain-tree. This animal is not a quarter of the size of the flying-fox, being only a foot and a half from tip to tip of the wings, consequently it is easily accommodated in a birdcage, and makes a pleasant pet. I once caught one with a net, as it was negotiating a guava to which it had no right, and in a short time it grew quite tame. When I presented a peeled plantain at the door of its cage it would travel along the wires, hanging by its feet and thumb-nails, and take the fruit out of my hand. Then it wrapped its wings round the plantain, and, beginning at one end, went steadily through it. The plantain was as big as itself, but capacity for food is one of the strong points of the whole bat family, and there was seldom anything left in the morning. During the day it enfolded itself in its wings and slept, hanging by one foot from the top of its cage.

Bats have one lovely virtue, and that is family affection. I shall never forget a captive family of demon bats which I once saw, the grim old papa, the mother perhaps a trifle more hideous, and the half-grown youngster, not quite able yet to provide for himself. There was something very touching in the tender attachment to one another of three such ill-omened objects. Fruit-bats, too, when they go foraging, never leave the baby at home. It clings to the mother's breast, and she carries it wherever she goes. A humane friend of mine has communicated to me, for insertion here, a very affecting story of a bat which he found, prostrate and bleeding, with a mob of dastardly crows seeking its life. Running to the rescue, he lifted it up, and discovered, under its wings, a helpless little infant, which it was vainly trying to save from its ruthless persecutors. The pathos of the story comes to a head at the point where my humane friend, putting his hand into his trousers' pocket, draws out two annas and gives them to a native lad, charging him to protect the poor creature and take it to a place of safety. No one who has any respect for his own feelings will press the matter further, and inquire what the native did when he had received the two annas and my humane friend was gone.

The Mysore Jungles
GEORGE PERESS SANDERSON

In the jungles the young grass commences to spring with the first showers in April, and by July has attained the height of a man. This is the case chiefly in hill tracts; in the low-country jungles it is more backward, as there is less rain and it is grazed down by cattle. By 'grass' in Indian jungles is meant the broad-bladed and long-leaved lemon-grass and other coarse kinds, which grow in large tufts; also reeds in swampy ground, and small ground-creepers. This season is the time par excellence for stalking and shooting large game. The animals are intent on the new supply of fodder; occasional rain makes tracking easy; and after May the sky is usually obscured by clouds and driving mist in the hills, and considerable exertion may be undergone without discomfort.

From July to January the grass is so high and thick that game cannot be got at in it, and many places where good sport is

Essay taken from: Sanderson, George Peress. *Thirteen Years Among the Wild Beasts of India: Their Haunts and Habits from Personal Observation; With an Account of the Modes of Capturing and Taming Elephants*, second edition (London: Wm. H. Allen & Co., Publishers to the Indian Office, 1879), pp. 9–18.

obtainable earlier then become impenetrable. Driven out by the wet and discomfort, and tormented by myriads of flies, many animals leave the high and close cover at this time for the lighter shelter and choicer grazing to be had amongst the young and tender grass on the outskirts; but they retreat readily to the grass jungles if disturbed.

By January the grass has all seeded and become dry, and it is then fired by the jungle-people. The hitherto impenetrable jungles are now reduced to clear forests of trees, interspersed with separate evergreen thickets. Moving about in such forests is rendered easy, but warm, work, the heat rising from the blackened earth under a tropical sun being very trying where the forest is not dense. The jungle-people burn the grass to admit of their gathering certain fruits and jungle-products, especially the gall-nut, used in tanning. This burning insures a supply of sweet grass as soon as showers fall on the fertilising ash.

During the months when the jungles are clear, the wanderings of the game are necessarily curtailed, not only by want of cover, but also of food and water. The herds of elephants, bison, and deer collect in moist and deep valleys where the grass is green, and fires do not enter. The difficulty of finding these secluded places however, is great, as they are in such heavy and moist jungles that the very few wild people's dwellings that do exist are seldom near them, and unless the sportsman is well equipped for a march into difficult country, away from supplies of all kinds, they are inaccessible. To any one ignorant of the extent of the wild animals' hot-weather retreats it seems almost magical, after experiencing the difficulty of finding them during that season, to observe how they reappear on all sides with the first rains.

It is a magnificent sight to see the jungles of a hill-range burning. Sometimes immense tracts are on fire at once, and at night give forth a lurid blaze which lights up the country for miles round. If the fire is near, the roaring noise is truly appalling, and impresses one with a sense of the dread power of the element. Huge billows of thick smoke, in which lighted grass and leaves are whirled forward, roll heavily and slowly along, whilst a sound as of incessant discharges of small-arms is caused by the bamboos and grass stalks exploding. The noise lulls and swells with every alternation in the breeze and in proportion to the thickness of the undergrowth. Long after the main conflagration has passed, isolated bamboo-clumps and dried trees are seen burning fiercely like pillars of flame, till they fall over with a sullen crash, and are quenched. Many trees smoulder for months. I knew one of enormous size, the roots of which, some of the girth of a bullock, or greater, burnt for three and a half years, the fire smouldering slowly underground in the roots long after the parent stem had fallen.

During the day countless buzzards and fly-catchers hover over the smoke, preying on the bewildered insects which are escaping from it. The destruction of noxious vermin by the fires must be considerable; but many animals and reptiles, as the land-tortoise and snakes, whose powers of speed do not enable them to escape by those means, survive by burying themselves in holes or burrows amongst rocks.

I have never seen jungle-fires advance at any great rate, except in very dry and long grass, unshaded by trees, and under the influence of a strong wind. Here burning leaves and hot ashes are carried far ahead of the main fire, and a fresh blaze starts up at once where they fall. I do not think jungle-fires ever travel four miles in an hour. The devouring element licks up all before it in some places with wonderful rapidity, but it seldom proceeds far without a check. Wild animals retreat before conflagrations; but many, as for instance herds of elephants encumbered with young, could not always escape if the fires travelled at any great rate. I have never known any animals, except a few young sambur, too young to walk far, to be caught in the fire; but jungle-people have been burnt on occasions. This has always occurred through their not heeding the danger, and staying to search for some near asylum, instead of at once starting for a known place of safety. Three men of a village near my camp in the Billiga-rungun hills, who were cutting bamboos, were burnt in this way, through not liking to leave their work further than the shelter of a ravine near, which proved insufficient to protect them from the wave of flame and smoke that passed over them.

Elephants, bison, &c., do not retreat straight before a fire, but to one side or the other. The fires seldom form a long front, so this outflanking movement readily succeeds. At the first distant crackle, or smell of smoke, wild animals at once retire. Fires are much less dangerous than is supposed if anything like prompt means are taken to effect a retreat. The jungle-people secure their houses by cutting some of the grass round, and firing it early in the season, before it is very dry. This stops the onward rush of the larger fires later on. Fires burn much more fiercely during the day than at night, as there is usually more wind, and everything is dry and brittle; whilst at night the heavy dews have a marked effect on the progress of the burning through making the grass damp ahead. The conflagrations are only fierce and general for one month, usually March; they begin in January.

A good deal is said in connection with forestry in India regarding the destructiveness of the annual fires to young trees, and attempts are constantly made, but rarely succeed, to exclude fires from reserved Government forests. It is, perhaps, doubtful whether they are so destructive as is believed, and whether the young plants of teak and other trees would flourish well if constantly choked and overshaded by undergrowth. At any rate there are splendid forests where, though fires have raged annually from time immemorial, the timber is as close as the ground can support it. The grass is not so high or thick under shade as in open ground, and as artificial teak nurseries are usually made in land from which the timber has been removed, and where, in consequence, grass grows apace, the fires are there more severe on the young plants than in their natural forests. There are always numerous young plants of timber-trees in every forest which can never live, as they grow more thickly than the ground can support when mature. The fittest survive; and though fires may scorch and shrivel up their leaves, I have not observed that the saplings which take root soon after the burning of one season are killed by the fires of the next, though many of those which are but a few months old when the fires commence are destroyed. I have been told by experienced jungle-men that timber-plants are burnt down for five or six consecutive years, the roots meanwhile thickening and strengthening underground, until they give birth to a plant sufficiently strong to withstand the effects of the momentary wave of flame.

The Mysore jungles may be divided into three classes. First, virgin forests of heavy timber, usually found in the hill-ranges along the borders of the province. They are naturally finest in such places as are inaccessible for the removal of timber; for from the more accessible parts the timber-supply of the country is drawn. The virgin forests are only inhabited by a few wild jungle-people. Secondly, the lighter belt of forest, usually about ten miles in width, intervening between the virgin forests and civilisation. From this tract the villagers procure the small timber and bamboos they require for household purposes. They also graze their cattle in it, seldom entering the heavier forest except during the hot weather, when pasturage elsewhere is very scarce. A few villages occur in this tract, but they are rather stations for cattle-grazing than for cultivation, nor are they often of a permanent nature. Thirdly, scrub-jungle of low and thorny bushes, which occurs at intervals throughout the open cultivated country in the sterile tracts, on the deserted sites of villages, &c. From this small firewood and bushes for fencing are obtained, and in it the cattle and flocks of the villagers in the interior are grazed.

In the heavy forests, elephants, bison, and sambur are the chief game. These animals come at certain seasons into the lighter belt. But the legitimate occupants of the latter are the tiger, panther, bear, spotted-deer, and wild hog. The wild dog ranges through both heavy and light forests, and is terribly destructive to the deer tribe; he is never found in open country. In the scrub-jungle, particularly in those tracts near detached hills and low ranges, panthers, leopards, bears, ravine deer, wolves, and sometimes antelope, are found. Antelope and wolves, however, chiefly confine themselves to large tracts of open uncultivated country, on the borders of which the ryots' crops furnish the former with superior grazing, and his flocks are often pounced upon by the latter.

The following gamc-list comprises all the animals found in Mysore, except monkeys, squirrels, mungooses, ant-eaters, lemurs, flying-foxes, rats, and other small animals not objects of sport—

List of Mysore Games

English.	Of Naturalist.*	In Canarese.	Remarks.
Elephant	Elephas indicus	Anay	Very numerous in border forests.
Bison or Gaur	Gaveus gaurus	Karti, Kard-yem-may, Kard-kor-na, Doddoo	Abundant throughout the ranges frequented by elephants.
Tiger	Felis tigris	Hooli	Plentiful in suitable localities.
Panther	Felis pardus	Dod-ibba	Less common than the leopard. A black variety is sparingly found in Mysore.

* Jerdon's Mammals of India.

English.	Of Naturalist.*	In Canarese.	Remarks.
Leopard	*Felis leopardus*	Kirba	Very common.
Cheetah or Hunting Leopard	*Felis jubata*	Chircha, Sivungi	Exceedingly rare in Mysore— almost unknown.
Bear	*Ursus labiatus*	Karadi	Plentiful in certain localities.
Wolf	*Canis pallipes*	Torla	Not numerous.
Striped Hyaena	*Hyaena straita*	Kat-kirba	Common.
Wild Dog	*Cuon rutilans*	Ken-naie, Kardnaie	Do.
Sambur	*Rusa aristotelis*	Kadavay	Common in the forest tracts.
Spotted-Deer	*Axis maculatus*	Sarga, Jati, Mikka	Very common.
Barking or Rib-faced Deer, Munt-jac, Kakur, Jungle-Sheep	*Cervulus aureus*	Kard or Kondkurri, Chali.	Common.
Indian Antelope	*Antilope bezoartica*	Hoolay-kara, Jinki	Not numerous.
Indian Gazelle or Ravine Deer	*Gazella bennettii*	Sunk-hoolay	Not common.
Wild Hog	*Sus indicus*	Kard-hundi, Curry-jati	Very numerous.
Crocodile	*Crocodilus indicus*	Mosalay	Not numerous, and seldom over ten feet long.
Jackal	*Canis aureus*	Nurrie	Very numerous.

* Jerdon's *Mammals of India.*

English.	Of Naturalist.*	In Canarese.	Remarks.
Fox	*Vulpes bengalensis*	Kemp-nurrie	Not very numerous.
Common Jungle-Cat	*Felis chaus*	Kard-bekkoo	Very common.
Leopard-Cat	*Felis bengalensis*	Bottina-bekkoo	Less common.
Otter	*Lutra nair*	Neer-naie	Plentiful.
Porcupine	*Hystrix leucura*	Mool-hundi	Do.
Mouse-Deer	*Memimna indica*	Koor-pundi	Do.
Hare	*Lepus nigricollis*	Molla	Do.

The following animals of Indian sport are not found in Mysore.

English.	Of Naturalist.*	In Canarese.	Remarks.
Rhinoceros	*Rhinoceros indicus*	None	Not found in Southern India.
Wild Buffalo	*Bubulus arni*	Do	
Neelgai	*Portax pictus*	Mayroo, Kard-kud-ray	Found in the Madras Presidency on the borders of Mysore.
Ibex, or the Neilgherry Wild Goat	*Hemitragus hylocrius*	Kard-ardoo	

Birds.—Jungle-fowl, pea-fowl, and spur-fowl are common in the woods; bustard, floriken, red-legged partridge, quail, and rock-grouse in the open country; and wild duck, teal, snipe, wild geese, flamingoes, pelicans, and cranes in the lakes and rice-fields. Doves of several varieties are common both in the woods and open country.

* Jerdon's *Mammals of India.*

Fish.—The rivers and artificial lakes in Mysore abound with excellent fish, but I have never succeeded in getting much sport with the fly. They may be taken by spinning or ground fishing—the latter chiefly at night. There is now in the museum at Bangalore the head and skin of a fish—a species of carp or *mahseer*, and called *billi*, or silver-fish, in Canarese—caught by me in 1871 in the Lutchmenteert, which measured 60 inches in length and 38 in girth. The circumference inside the mouth when caught was 24 inches. I was unfortunately unable to weigh this fish, but I estimated it by rough tests at not less than 100 lb. I have seen much larger fish, without doubt upwards of 150 lb., caught by natives, chiefly by netting during the months when the rivers are low. At such times two or three villages of professional fishermen will combine to net a single large fish known to be a prisoner in a pool during the hot weather. The pool may be a hundred yards long and broad, and the water fifteen feet deep, with cavernous rocks capable of sheltering fish; but by joining their nets, and diving and working for two or three days, they seldom fail to secure the prize.

The few crocodiles that are found in the Mysore rivers very rarely attack people; and fishermen—who pay no heed to them—have told me that if they come upon a crocodile whilst following their employment, it will skulk at the bottom and not move though handled, apparently believing it escapes observation. Crocodiles are, like all wild creatures, very timid where not encouraged, as is sometimes done by superstitious natives. Incredible though it may seem to readers with no knowledge of the saurians but that derived from stories of their boldness elsewhere, I may instance having seen several *bestas* (the professional boatmen, divers, and fishermen of Mysore) dive time after time into water twelve feet deep, and bring to the surface by the tail a crocodile seven feet long which I had wounded. The creature was not in any way crippled, but seemed overcome with fear. It offered no resistance till dragged near a rock where I stood with a rope, when it would turn and snap at the man pulling it, always sinking, however, the moment this demonstration made him let go its tail. Different divers went down successively, one at a time, and brought it to the surface; I at last killed it with a charge of shot.

Whilst in pursuit of game in the Mysore forests I have often been struck with wonder at the remains of the dwellings and works of a bygone population which are to be found, now engulfed in jungle. The whole country bears traces of having once been better populated than at present, and many of the remains are of a character that speak of the industry and culture of its inhabitants. Some of the temples, monuments, and sculptures are as grand in conception as they are admirable in execution. The old irrigation works of the country, consisting of stone dams across the rivers, often many hundred yards in length, and composed of blocks far beyond any of the native appliances of the present day to deal with; canals; and reservoirs, or lakes; mark the material prosperity of the country ages ago. Granite of excellent quality is found throughout the country, and the extensive use of this imperishable material in the old structures has preserved them intact to the present time. Wherever a village of importance existed remains of interest are to be seen. The sportsman wandering in the forest is often tempted to rest on his rifle, and muse sadly over the scenes of former life and industry, where the voices are now hushed, and wild Nature, deprived of her dominion for a few short years, again reigns supreme. The elephant rests at mid-day under the sacred peepul-tree, once in the centre of the village, where old and young met at evening—the former to discuss village matters and rest after the fatigues of the day; the latter to amuse themselves, thoughtless of the future. Where are they now? Broken images and disused querns lie around; the wells are choked and dry; bears and panthers find shelter in the very temples where offerings were presented to the village gods, and where festivals were held. But the people have passed away without other record than the jungle-overgrown ruins, which have defied time. And may not similar changes follow again? Where the sportsman now tracks the elephant and tiger, cultivation may smile and happy voices be heard long after his own insignificant existence is more effectually forgotten tlian that of the people over whose traces he now muses.

Amongst scenes whither my duty or pleasure led me, I always felt particular interest in a portion of the Hoonsoor jungles which lies within the watershed of the Cubbany river. A chain of ancient channels here forms a wonderful system of irrigation, but they have caused the ruin of the land they once fertilised.

Often as I sat and overlooked the unbroken stretch of jungle which had swallowed up the country did I speculate on its former condition, and the causes that had led to the change. These seem evident. The whole tract must have been comparatively healthy at one time, as the remains of large towns testify to its former population; it must then have been open country, as cities do not spring up in jungle-encumbered tracts in India. The people, however, sighed for water to increase the fertility of their land, dependent upon rainfall alone, and a remarkable physical feature placed an unlimited supply of the fertilising element at their command. The valley which contains the channels runs nearly due west to east, and is about twenty miles long by five broad. From its upper or west end to its termination on the Cubbany river to the east, there is a fall of probably 500 feet. At the upper end, just over the watershed ridge and not more than 50 feet below it, flows the Lutchmenteert river, a considerable stream in the rainy season, and never quite dry; its course here is approximately from south to north, and it is within half a mile of the ridge. The former inhabitants of the valley to the east had cut a channel through the ridge, and introduced Lutchmenteert water into the Cubbany vale.

With water thus available on the top of the watershed, irrigation was practically unlimited, and channels were led contouring along each side of the valley at a high level for many miles. The drainage water of these was caught up again and again by tanks or artificial lakes thrown across the valley.

These mighty works, though in ruins, still bear testimony to the former ability and industry of the inhabitants. But the fertilising element which now surrounded them became the means of their extinction. Land not cultivated must soon have been overgrown with rank jungle, nurtured by the moisture. The culturable area, too, must have been gradually reduced by about four-fifths, as irrigated land produces so much more valuable crops, and its cultivation is so much more arduous, that a small portion of what each man cultivated before as dry land would now suffice for his wants and engage all his labour.

Thus, each community in the valley found itself gradually shut in by jungle and rank herbage instead of the former open land. The whole valley became permeated with moisture, and the exhalations from the ground caused malarial fevers which eventually depopulated it, and which at this day prevent its reoccupation. The sites of the chief towns are now only marked by overgrown and weather-beaten earth-work fortifications, or by stone temples of a solidity that has defied the ravages of time; and all traces of many smaller villages have been lost.

The largest of the towns in the valley was Rutnapoori-korte (the City of Rubies), and it is probably at least 150 years since the last inhabitants left it. There are some granite slabs engraved in old Canarese characters near a fine old temple which covers a large area, and these probably contain some account of the founding or history of the temple. The temple is composed of massive pillars and beams of solid granite, many of which have fallen and lie strewn around. I learnt from the legends of the surrounding country that seven sisters formerly lived in Rutnapoori. These were the concubines of the rajah of the place, and each chose a site for the construction of a lake in the valley. These seven tanks, three of them now breached, are named after the sisters. The lowest of the seven was built by the youngest, and has the advantage of catching the surplus water from the others. It is still a splendid sheet of water, called Kurrigul, near the road from Mysore to Manantoddy in the Wynaad country. This road passes through the lower portion of the valley, running parallel with the Cubbany river; and, as the country is more open and accessible here, several large villages and patches of cultivation which had never quite died out have been resuscitated, and are extending.

For the upper portion of the valley, overgrown with dense unwholesome forest, nothing can be done at present. Population has long since moved elsewhere, and the tract is not yet required for producing food. A few hamlets spring up occasionally, as some small capitalist is tempted by the richness of the land, and the easy terms on which it is obtainable from Government, to cultivate a portion. But the wretched ryots who undertake the work live in a miserable condition. They are soon affected with enlarged spleens, the invariable accompaniment of fevers induced by a bad climate and bad water, and either give up, or decamp with the advances of money they have received. These spasmodic attempts at reclamation seldom last long. The capitalist finds the advantages of the soil are counterbalanced by the difficulty of the position. As long as it is sought to establish villages in the valley far below the level of the upper channels and their cultivation, so long must failure follow, as the unhealthiness of the locality is insurmountable. The only thing possible would be to restore the chain of tanks in the valley, and to abandon the cultivation the heights. The tanks could be filled once or twice a-year from the Lutchmenteert, and, the upper cultivation being abandoned, the sides of the valley would not be pervaded with moisture. The breezes would be more healthy, and the villages cultivating the land below the tanks would be above the level of the dampness, and some portion of the former salubrity of the place would be restored. As long as water is kept running at a high level and drenching the soil, the bottom of the jungle-encumbered valley must be inimical to human life.

The land below the high-level channels has, however, been largely reclaimed during the past ten years. The cultivators live in Hoonsoor and adjacent villages, not in the tract itself, only visiting it for the purpose of cultivation. The low grounds in the valley are given up to the grazing of the Commissariat cattle at Hoonsoor, and this is the best use, perhaps, they can now be put to. These grazing grounds are essential in different places over the country, and there is usually enough cultivable land available without invading them.

Notes on Contributors

Jay Mazoomdaar is an independent journalist and filmmaker. He exposed the extermination of tigers from Sariska Tiger Reserve and National Park.

Krupakar and Senani have done extensive research on the dhole for over a decade and produced films on them for channels like National Geographic and Animal Planet, which won many awards worldwide, including the Panda 2010 for 'Animal Behaviour', the first ever for an Asian filmmaker.

Kartik Shanker is a sea turtle specialist working on community ecology and biogeography. He is a faculty member at the Centre for Ecological Sciences, Indian Institute of Science, Bangalore.

Rauf Ali is an eminent wildlife ecologist. He is the founding trustee of the Foundation for Ecological Research, Advocacy and Learning.

Madhusudan Katti is a reconciliation ecologist and associate professor of Vertebrate Biology at California State University, Fresno.

Yash Veer Bhatnagar is a conservation biologist with keen interest in Himalayan wildlife and is a senior scientist with the Nature

Conservation Foundation, Mysore, and the Snow Leopard Trust, Seattle.

Ananda Banerjee is a conservation journalist, graphic designer and fine art photographer. An avid birder he is the author of the best-selling *Common Birds of the Indian Subcontinent*, *Wild Trail in Madhya Pradesh* and contributing author for *Birds and People*.

Hugh Allen served in the British army during the Second World War, but when a bad head wound put him out of active service in 1942, he was hospitalized in India. He learnt to love the country and took up farming amongst the jungles, developing his skills for big-game shooting out of necessity, rather than entertainment.

Edward Lockwood served in the Bengal Civil Service and was the magistrate of Monghyr (now written as Munger in Bihar).

Frank Finn was an ornithologist. He was the editor of the *Avicultural Magazine* in 1909–10 and the Finn's weaver is named after him.

Richard Lydekker was an English naturalist and paleontologist. He was associated with the Geological Survey of India from 1874–82.

Captain James Forsyth was an officer of the Bengal Staff Corps who became one of the first Europeans to explore Satpura.

Edward Hamilton Aitken was a civil servant in India and a founding member of the Bombay Natural History Society. He was well known by the pen name of Eha.

George Peress Sanderson was a civil servant who introduced a novel way of catching wild elephants for subsequent taming and training in forestry work.

Acknowledgements

This book would not have been possible without the support of two dear friends, Kapish Mehra and Jay Mazoomdar. A special 'thank you' to all the contributors. I would also like to thank Sneha Gusain for her suggestions and editorial expertise at Rupa Publications.

www.ingramcontent.com/pod-product-compliance
Lightning Source LLC
Chambersburg PA
CBHW070920270326
41927CB00011B/2653